UBUNTU

ENDORSEMENTS

The five P's of *ubuntu* displayed in this book should be considered for effective workplaces. Vuyisile Msila has reconceptualised management and leadership in the workplace. *Ubuntu*-driven approaches have never been so relevant as they are today for thriving organisations.

Prof Mishack Gumbo, (IKS Specialist),
University of South Africa

This book comes at a critical time in the country, when leadership is failing the citizens of South Africa. *Ubuntu: shaping the current workplace with (African) wisdom* is an ideal reference book for all leaders and managers. Msila tackles a very powerful word, *ubuntu*, giving clear directions on how it can be used in a working environment; which makes this book useful in corporate as well as government departments.

Mangaliso Buzani, Writer & Artist, Imbizo Arts of South Africa

This very powerful book has to be the most definitive work I have read to date on the concept of *ubuntu* and what it means in the workplace. This is a truly seminal book that is a must-read for anyone hoping to implement and embed the African philosophy of *ubuntu* into their organisation. It offers a comprehensive and compelling theoretical range of underpinnings, with practical wisdom on how to make it work.

Prof Shirley Zinn, CEO Shirley Zinn Consulting and Non- Executive Director
and Trustee of Boards and Trusts

In *Ubuntu: Shaping the current workplace with (African) wisdom* Prof Msila has succeeded admirably in explaining the essence of *ubuntu*, but more importantly, shown its use and applicability to improving today's organisations. It is a most readable book and is recommended.

Dave van Eeden, editor of The Role of the Chief Human Resources Officer
and independent consultant

One can just listen to the stories of Africa to become aware of the wisdom that filters through in the oral history of the narrative people of this continent. Strong discipline and astuteness underpin the integrated philosophy of *ubuntu*.

Organisations seldom succeed in unleashing these indigenous insights and being-ness for the benefit of the collective. Deep in the roots of *ubuntu*, humane, principled and value-driven strength can be discovered. Insights into how social systems really function can be remembered. By integrating our roots, we can bring spiritedness and humaneness back to organisational spaces that have, over years, become mechanical and task-driven to the exclusion of integration. Maybe the world can find the key to solving organisational and societal problems in Africa, and in the ways of its people.

Prof Vuyisile Msila masterfully explores how the *ubuntu* way of being can sustainably influence organisational doing. In this important contribution, he succeeds in offering a wise, yet practical approach that will ensure that the old African ways are not forgotten.

Dr Rica Viljoen, Managing Director, Mandala Consulting

This new book on *Ubuntu in the workplace*, through an analysis of various aspects of the philosophy, contextual relevance and practices of people-centred workplaces, as well as a wide range of examples, demonstrates both current challenges in diversity management and future opportunities for change. It does this succinctly by advocating a unique approach to creating more inclusive organisations based on lessons learnt from both traditional and futuristic African wisdom. The theoretical foundation and practical examples presented in this book illustrate the diversity and richness of current approaches of creating more human workplaces in order to meet individual, organisational and societal expectations. From its balanced mix of chapters emphasising diverse approaches and practices from the cultural richness of the philosophy of *ubuntu*, readers will be able to derive important lessons, African wisdoms, as well as clear guidelines for establishing people-driven organisations.

Marius Meyer, CEO: SA Board for People Practices (SABPP)

Copyright © Knowres Publishing and Prof Vuyisile Msila

All reasonable steps have been taken to ensure that the contents of this work do not, directly or indirectly, infringe any existing copyright of any third person and, further, that all quotations or extracts taken from any other publication or work have been appropriately acknowledged and referenced. The publisher, editors and printers take no responsibility for any copyright infringement committed by an author of this work.

Copyright subsists in this work. No part of this work may be reproduced in any form or by any means without the written consent of the publisher or the authors.

While the publisher, editors and printers have taken all reasonable steps to ensure the accuracy of the contents of this work, they take no responsibility for any loss or damage suffered by any person as a result of that person relying on the information contained in this work.

First published in 2015

ISBN: 978-1-86922-559-9
eISBN: 978-1-86922-560-5 (PDF eBook)

Published by Knowres Publishing (Pty) Ltd
P O Box 3954
Randburg
2125
Republic of South Africa

Tel: (011) 706-6009
Fax: (011) 706-1127
E-mail: orders@knowres.co.za
Website: www.kr.co.za

Printed and bound: Mega Digital (Pty) Ltd. Parow Industria, Cape Town
Typesetting, layout and design: Cia Joubert, cia@knowres.co.za
Cover design: Stick SA, Mpotseng@sticksa.co.za
Editing and proofreading: Mandy Collins, mcollins@icon.co.za
Project management: Cia Joubert, cia@knowres.co.za
Index created with: TExtract, www.Texyz.com

UBUNTU

Shaping the current workplace with (African) wisdom

Vuyisile Msila

2015

Table of Contents

About the author ------- iii

Preface ------- iv

Foreword ------- ix

1. *Chapter one:* **Workplaces using *ubuntu*** ------- 1
   - 1.1 Introduction and background ------- 1
   - 1.2 What *ubuntu* is not ------- 3
   - 1.3 Explaining *ubuntu* ------- 4
   - 1.4 Change and levels of maturity ------- 7
   - 1.5 *Ubuntu* and the need for servant leadership ------- 13

2. *Chapter two:* **People-centredness** ------- 17
   - 2.1 Introduction ------- 17
   - 2.2 People-centred workplace culture ------- 20
   - 2.3 Empowering people – *Ubuntu* African values ------- 22
   - 2.4 Transformational leadership ------- 24
   - 2.5 Mentoring, *ubuntu* and people-centredness ------- 26
   - 2.6 Shared vision ------- 33
   - 2.7 The organisation is about us, not you! ------- 34

3. *Chapter three:* **Permeable walls** ------- 37
   - 3.1 Introduction ------- 37
   - 3.2 Openness and honesty: supporting relationships ------- 39
   - 3.3 Barriers of communication ------- 43
   - 3.4 Direction of the organisation ------- 45

4. *Chapter four:* **Partisanship** ------- 47
   - 4.1 Introduction ------- 47
   - 4.2 Building loyalty through organisational values ------- 51
   - 4.3 Qualities displayed by loyal employees ------- 54
   - 4.4 Leader/manager loyalty – I am because of this community ------- 56

| | | 4.5 | Shared moral values and loyalty | 58 |

5.	*Chapter five:* **Progeny**			**61**
	5.1	Introduction		61
	5.2	Strengthening relationships and solidarity		64
	5.3	Sharing power		65
	5.4	Mutual understanding		65
	5.5	Building better teams		66
	5.6	Using humanness to chase a vision		69

6.	*Chapter six:* **Production**		**71**
	6.1	Introduction	71
	6.2	*Ubuntu* and performance at work	73
	6.3	Strong organisational values	78
	6.4	Improving workplace culture and the role of the leader	79
	6.5	Time management	83
	6.6	Investing in development/training	85
	6.7	SOAR the winning organisation	87
	6.8	Power of delegation	90
	6.9	Emotional intelligence	92
	6.10	Maturity summit	93

7.	*Chapter seven:* **Conclusion**		**99**
	7.1	Concluding comments	99
	7.2	Building a community	102
	7.3	Professional maturity and *ubuntu*	103
	7.4	Learning and sustenance of *ubuntu*	104

References	106
Endnotes	111
Index	117

About the Author

Vuyisile Msila is a professor and head at Unisa's Institute for African Renaissance Studies. He leads a number of interdisciplinary and multidisciplinary research projects, although his special interests are general leadership as well as African models in leadership and management.

He has conducted extensive work in leadership research in educational institutions, and was also a member of the Zenex/ACE research team that worked nationally, evaluating the Advanced Certificate in Education – School Management and Leadership. This was a project commissioned by the Department of Basic Education.

He has also developed a few theories on organisational development and sustenance, and this book explores one of the models that Msila has developed on *ubuntu* and leadership.

Msila serves as an editorial board member for *Mevlana International Journal, Educational Reform Journal, Journal of Educational Research and Studies* and *Universal Journal of Psychology*.

Preface

Over the years I have worked closely with managers who were passionate about improving their spaces as they attempted to create efficient organisations. This has led me to explore what elements made some organisations succeed while others failed.

Among the areas I have conducted research in was the use of *ubuntu* leadership in enhancing workplace performance. This was an attempt to see what leaders can learn from the oldest African philosophy that has been practised in various African countries. However, while conducting research in some organisations, I discovered how leadership and management issues tend to be universal.

Therefore this book looks at how we can improve workplaces by using the old values and wisdom of our forebears.

There is a need to visualise the village, where the community was guided by seemingly basic human principles that had deep implications for the village's survival. While we may often speak of *ubuntu*, we do not always understand what it entails. This book illustrates how leaders and managers can use the wisdom from this old African philosophy, sometimes loosely referred to as African humanism.

Communities or villages (represented by organisations in this book) will not thrive unless the king, queen or chief at the helm has a vision for the people. We are at a time when organisations need wise leaders and managers, or their organisation will falter. Frequently, we constantly enforce only the rational approaches to management.

Peters and Waterman,[1] who have written extensively on management, state that professionalism in management is regularly equated with 'hard headed rationality'. However, these authors argue that although the rationalist approaches teach people that well-trained, professional managers can manage anything, these approaches miss some arguments. Yet, another author, Bottery,[2] writes about the need to have moral leaders to guide institutions if people are to have a moral society.

The importance of aspects such as culture and norms has been underscored by numerous leaders in South Africa and in other parts of the world. Other leaders have perceived subjective qualities like spirituality as important factors in guiding effective organisations. Successful leaders state that getting culture right and paying attention to how other stakeholders define and experience meaning are two widely accepted rules for creating effective organisations[3].

Sergiovanni also contends:

> Culture is generally thought of as the normative glue that holds a particular organisation together. With shared visions, values, and beliefs at its heart, culture serves as a compass setting, steering people in a common direction. It provides norms that govern the way people interact with each other. It provides a framework for deciding what does or does not make sense.

The above shows how crucial culture is within an organisation and that the leader's role is important in refining this culture. Some research has shown the importance of certain African models in guiding not only successful but also highly moral organisations.

Many authors have highlighted the need for an *ubuntu* approach in leadership. Mthembu[4] describes *ubuntu* as the key to all African values, saying that it involves humanness, a good disposition towards others, and a moral nature. Furthermore, Mthembu[5] says that *ubuntu* describes the significance of group solidarity and interdependence in African culture.

Lovemore Mbigi,[6] who is an expert in this area, supports this by pointing out that *ubuntu* is a metaphor that describes the significance of group solidarity on issues that are vital to the survival of African communities. The constant calls for a moral society are desperate calls for society to embrace this solidarity as it changes for the better.

Mbigi[7] points out that fears and uncertainties are characteristic of transition and it is the task of leadership to manage the fears of the people. *Ubuntu* is envisaged as a philosophy that would ensure that there is more diligence and a culture of achievement.

A South African Department of Education publication[8] points out that:

> Equality might require us to put up with people who are different, non-sexism and non-racism might require us to rectify the inequities of the past, but *ubuntu* goes much further: it embodies the concept of mutual understanding and the active appreciation of the value of human difference ... Ultimately; *ubuntu* requires you to respect others if you are to respect yourself.

In a society that has been made complex by a number of social issues, the philosophy of *ubuntu* encounters many social currents that flow in various directions. Some of these create obstacles that may oppose the spread of *ubuntu*.

The cultural activist Pitika Ntuli[9] states that the spirit of *ubuntu* has long disappeared and that is why we need an African renaissance. Furthermore, Ntuli[10] argues that in the face of the present cultural and moral collapse in South Africa, there is a need to strive for a rebirth. Yet, Mvume Dandala[11] states that *ubuntu* requires a great deal of learning and sharing and institutions can achieve this through the training of people to practise greater interaction. Organisations and the communities around them need to learn the values of *ubuntu*.

In this book I look at what I refer to as five P's of *ubuntu*, namely:

People-centredness	Permeable walls	Partisanship	Progeny	Production

I explain how these can improve workplaces because they contain the elements that enable communities/villages to be improved. The objective is to illustrate how workplaces can be enhanced, thus making them successful. This is also useful for underperforming organisations.

Effective managers and leaders can change even ingrained cultures when they arrive at organisations where employees have internalised beliefs detrimental to organisational development. It may take long depending on the qualities of an organisation. But matured, professional and effective leaders can change organisations for the better. *Ubuntu*-driven approaches can make a big difference.

Lastly, I would like to point out that in March-April 2015 we saw xenophobic attacks on foreign nationals in KwaZulu-Natal and in some parts of Gauteng. Many argued that *ubuntu* is dead in South Africa. Indeed this created a huge concern in South Africa and the neighbouring African states. Yet, the fact that this did not spread to all provinces may be an indication that there is a glimmer of hope; that *ubuntu* is still alive. Moreover, civil society, religious organisations, government departments and businesses came out voicing their condemnation of the xenophobic attacks. The age old principles of this philosophy will sustain better working communities and a strong nation.

Vuyisile Msila
Head: Institute for African Renaissance Studies
University of South Africa
College of Graduate Studies
287 Nana Sita Street
Pretoria

FOREWORD

South Africa and other nation states have witnessed a history that was characterised by a strict focus on production in the workplace at the expense of sound human relations between the leadership and the led. The drive to meet contractual obligations occupied the mind of the leader or manager, who thus treated employees as objects rather than human beings. Unfortunately, this disjuncture between production-driven leadership and human relations still persists to a larger degree even in contemporary democratic societies.

In this book Msila attempts to draw our attention to the metaphor of *ubuntu* as a possible approach that can be utilised in magnifying human relations while production is not compromised. Msila uses the extended metaphor of a village and community when he refers to organisations and with this he is able to spell out the strength in *ubuntu* philosophy and management. His wealth of experience accumulated through conducting organisational development research enhances his skills in writing about *ubuntu* in organisations. In this book he suggests the practical ways in which *ubuntu* can be used to grow the organisation.

Msila suggests a strategy based on the five Ps – *People-centredness, Permeable Walls, Partisanship, Progeny* and *Production*, to help him carve and suggest solutions to current workplace challenges. From an *ubuntu* perspective, this strategy will ensure care, respect, tolerance, kinship, share vision, partnership, conversations, and so on, which will in turn ensure the expected production. This also calls for the redesign of contractual obligations so that they accommodate *ubuntu*-centred ethos. Production levels may be pushed high by the workers' willingness to commit if they notice that the leadership does take their needs into account. This calls for a new approach towards work – 'we-centredness' which favours approaching work from a community of workers' perspective, rather than 'I-centredness' which prioritises only the manager's or leader's goal list.

This book provides one of the transformational resources that would make workplaces satisfying rather than burdensome.

Prof Mishack T Gumbo
Department of Science and Technology Education
University of South Africa
College of Education
Pretoria
0003

CHAPTER ONE

WORKPLACES USING *UBUNTU*

1.1 Introduction and background

Writing about *ubuntu* has become a challenging exercise if we consider how the word has been intentionally abused in some quarters, and unconsciously misused in others. There are so many instances today where people misconstrue the deep values enshrined in this old concept.

It is an old African concept, a way of life that was like religion in African societies long before the days of colonisation. It shows that one lives for others. It illustrates that if I have a cow and have milk every day, I share the milk with a fellow villager who has nothing. *Ubuntu* means sacrificing for others selflessly, caring and protecting fellow human beings. It is based on a premise that clearly points out that everything in my environment is crucial for my existence as well as that of fellow human beings.

The way of life in *ubuntu* conjures up the idea of a community in the workplace. This way of life demonstrates that for work to be done effectively, there needs to be some relationship among employees, and employees would in turn enhance the organisation as they engender team unity and solidarity. Individuals will exercise their creativity and initiatives but even this will be done with the success of the team or the community in mind.

In this regard, excellence is not promoted for negative competition. In several workplaces, people may want to prosper as fellow workers are stunted on the lowest rung. When workers operate within the paradigm of *ubuntu*, though, they know what they do is part of interconnectedness.

Ubuntu is the antithesis of isolationism and exclusion. As many workplaces like schools, government departments and huge firms falter, it might be *ubuntu* that is required to revitalise these workplaces. Effective leaders will cultivate *ubuntu* in their workplaces.

Frequently, employees complain of rigid workplaces which have all the negative qualities such as:

- Individualism
- Self-importance
- Negative competition
- Disregard for morality
- Seeing others in terms of production
- An uncaring space that disregards relationships and well-being.

Yet all these are overcome by *ubuntu*'s qualities of community. Caring workplaces will understand some of challenges that employees encounter in their day-to-day operations. A manager in an *ubuntu* environment appreciates what each member brings to the community and gives support when employees are not adequate in carrying out their duties.

The idea of a workplace that is also a community implies a number of positive qualities:

- Interconnectedness
- Dependability
- Caring
- Team work
- Being led by a collective vision.

The community in an *ubuntu*-inspired workplace will have all these and more, and the community needs them for survival.

This book looks at this concept through a theory I have developed over the years. The Five Ps of *ubuntu* are factors that I suggest need to be engendered in any progressive workplace. The book demonstrates aspects that sustain *ubuntu* and how these can be spread in workplaces.

Ubuntu cannot be regarded as a panacea; a silver bullet in toxic workplaces. However, with the support of a conscientious community of workers and enhancing values, *ubuntu* will prosper. It is a way of life that sustained families, communities and chiefdoms in Africa, a philosophy that underscored values reinforcing the state of being human, among others. It is a way of life that magnifies the importance of living together, as this book will demonstrate.

1.2 What *ubuntu* is not

When I was a school teacher, I passed my principal's office one day and a colleague, Ben, came out grumbling and reeking of alcohol. "This School Governing Body does not have *ubuntu*," he blubbered. "They have recommended that I be suspended because I am reckless!" He staggered away from me, continuing: "*Abanabuntu aba bantu!*" (These people do not have *ubuntu!*)

However, little did Ben say about continually acting in an irresponsible manner at work. He was the one who had no *ubuntu*. For many days, his pupils in the agricultural science class sat without a teacher to teach them. While the teacher was in a nearby bar, the pupils sat with no hope to improve their future. The teacher did not display *ubuntu* to hundreds of families, mostly poor, who needed their children to succeed in order to change the poverty cycle. *Ubuntu* is not so senseless that it does not acknowledge the lack of commitment to the life of others. Therefore *ubuntu* is not a kind of *laissez faire*.

There are also those who think that if they know about *ubuntu* and its principles or they were born in a certain way, they cannot be accused of not having *ubuntu*. Yet *ubuntu* is not always innate, it does not only exist in intellect but is a way of life within a community. It is a practice that needs to be evident, and guided by values that people embrace. People may learn these within a community.

Finally, people may think that *ubuntu* is opposed to competition and excellence. Some might hold the notion that it encourages people to achieve mediocrity because they are concerned with fellow human beings. This is not so. In the African village, the people celebrated the best wrestlers, the best stick fighters, the best cooks, the best runners and so on. Yet, even these excellent villagers were celebrated within the context of their village. Their excellence was brilliance ascribed to the village. Therefore, *ubuntu* is not opposed to competition when competition promotes the community values and excellence. The victory may be an individual's but the glory is shared by the entire community. *Ubuntu* seeks to bring out the best in people.

1.3 Explaining *ubuntu*

The importance of the concept of *ubuntu* has become prominent under the democratic dispensation in South Africa. It is rooted in African traditional society and philosophy and it means humanness or the quality of being human. It espouses the ideal of interconnectedness among people as highlighted above.

In Africa there was always this belief that one lives for others. That one's life can be as fulfilling as it is for fellow humans. Children are not brought up by their biological parents only, but by the entire village.

There are so many idioms and phrases in various African languages that show the essence of this *ubuntu*. The Xhosa people who are a part of the Nguni group say,

Intaka yakha ngoboya benye translated as:

"A bird builds with the other (bird's) feathers."

Isandla sihlamba esinye translated as:

"Each hand washes the other."

These phrases refer to one crucial *ubuntu* factor: that people need one another to exist. Many African languages reflect this humanness, this interdependence among people. *Ubuntu* is based on these principles. It is grounded on the notion that life is a web of interconnectedness.

Based on democratic principles as well as the ethos of the African worldview, *ubuntu* is always described or presupposed to be an ideal democratic principle. The democratic ideals it enshrines appear to be enough to convince many that its democratic foundation has the potential to ease many societal problems. Currently, in South Africa, there is the quest for a new identity that is not like the identities based on race and colour of the past; this multicultural society seeks solutions from a number of democratic philosophies and models. In the past decade there has been a need to embrace the spirit of *ubuntu* in various aspects of the society.

Ntuli[12] says that the spirit of *ubuntu* has long disappeared; continuing that this is why there is a need for an African renaissance. Furthermore, Ntuli[13] says that in the face of the present cultural and moral collapse in South Africa, there is a need to strive for this African rebirth. The moral collapse in society may be the indication that *ubuntu* is marginalised by society.

Arguably, failing workplaces may have to inject *ubuntu* into their daily practice. Effective managers strive to improve their management strategies continually to ensure that their organisations reap from the experience of well-run organisations.

Lesiba Teffo[14], an academic who has written extensively on *ubuntu* and other African models, states that the principle of *ubuntu* has to be transmitted into management practice. He explains:

> There has to be a change in the mind-sets, a paradigm shift of thought processes, attitudes, old styles of management and human relations in the workforce ... Ubuntu is a value system that can be taught. It needs more than conceptual analysis. It must be disseminated through varied strata by the workplace. Ubuntu is not irreconcilable or offensive to affirmative change. The company must be prepared to address the whole climate. The process should avoid emphasising differences.

The paradigm shift that Teffo[15] discusses above means that people need to learn to embrace each other. *Ubuntu* thrives when there is consensus, democracy and dependence on one another. When people do not think as part of a unified community that has principles, they cannot have *ubuntu*. Selfishness, pride and magnified ego cannot build progressive workplaces where success is highlighted and human relations are supreme.

Furthermore, those who practise *ubuntu* philosophy demonstrate some form of maturity, a transcendental outlook on life in general. They can teach other community members while they also learn from everyday encounters. In workplaces, *ubuntu* practices enhance work ethics due to solidarity and team approaches.

Arguably, the values embraced by *ubuntu* are the missing links in dysfunctional workplaces. Unnecessary competition and apathy have led to employees not caring about fellow workers as employees may emphasise the "I" instead of "Us" or "We". This calls for growth within people so that they can be receptive to certain strategies that seek to bring positive change in an organisation.

Below, the focus is on John C. Maxwell's[16] theory of professional growth which I later link to *ubuntu*'s creation and sustenance. Maxwell[17] is an American author who has several books that focus on the development of leadership and growing organisations.

Chapter 1: Workplaces using *ubuntu*

1.4 Change and levels of maturity

Maxwell[18] maintains that for ideal change to happen in leadership there needs to be growth within the people working in an organisation. Some innovations in leadership will need people to buy in and then adopt them.

Maxwell[19] developed a model that demonstrates levels of growth in people within an organisation. People can only be effective change agents when they are able to perceive the need for change. According to Maxwell[20], there are five levels necessary in the accomplishment of leadership. Below these are presented in a descending form:

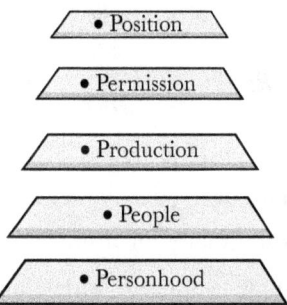

Leadership is enhanced as one ascends the levels from *Personhood Level* to *Position Level*. For leadership to remain effective, the leader should have strong followership. Leaders should not move alone otherwise there will be split interests within the groups they lead.

Furthermore, Maxwell[21] contends that there are two important aspects that people in organisations need to know. Firstly, they need to know the level they are on at a given moment. Secondly, the members of an organisation should know and apply the characteristics required for success to be attained at each level.

Below are some of the qualities crucial in each level as cited from Maxwell[22]:

Level one: Position/Rights

- knowing the job description
- being aware of the organisation's background
- accepting responsibility
- doing more than expected
- offering creative ideas for change.

Level two: Permission/Relationships

- possessing genuine love for people
- seeing through other people's eyes
- including others in your journey.

Level three: Production/Results

- initiating and accepting responsibility for growth
- developing and following a statement of purpose
- developing accountability for results
- becoming a change agent and understanding timing.

Level four: People development

- realising people are a most valuable asset
- being a model to others
- placing priority on developing people
- exposing key leaders to growth opportunities.

Level five: Personhood/Respect

- your followers are loyal and sacrificial
- you have spent years mentoring and moulding leaders
- you have become a consultant and are sought by others
- you transcend the organisation.

The theory above relies on oneness and understanding among workers. It shares a number of aspects with *ubuntu*. *Ubuntu* is one philosophy that has been upheld by many proactive Africans. It encompasses the emancipation of self and the acceptance of others. Yet, such philosophies, after years of cultural exclusion and support of exclusively Western models in society, have been relegated to the back. Mkandawire[23] argues that there have been barriers that have hindered the internalisation and progress of African ideals; these include authoritarianism, dependence and projects driven by power hunger and self-aggrandisement.

Teffo[24] points out that all that companies need is a mentor to teach or preach *ubuntu*, and this will go a long way towards answering the question of: "How do we incorporate *ubuntu* into our management style?"

The idea of introducing a mentor is critical, especially when one looks at the crucial aspect of preparing the workers for a climate conducive to being receptive to *ubuntu* models. With regards co-operation, Teffo[25] points out:

> *Ubuntu empowers people to love and respect each other. In the search for a new management style, the writing of memos may have to be supplemented by communication (follow-up oral presentation and/or discussions). It would yield better results if the director or manager were to go to the people and discuss issues with them.*

It is important to note that in many workplaces managers may struggle to incorporate *ubuntu* in a world devoid of certain values and morals as Ntuli[26] points out above. Colonisation has led to many ills in society and new values of greed.

Employees may not be certain what to do when they are supposed to act independently in leading teams. Many employees may not be used to decision-making and being creators of other leaders in an organisation. In my previous research in organisational development and management a few older employees would relate how they were used to "top-down" approaches, where information moved in a linear manner from head offices to the managers to the employees. These employees would also tell how they were paralysed when they were supposed to use creativity in their organisations and be self-driven.

This may be why Teffo[27] states that two reasons are important for a major paradigm shift in management theory and practice in South Africa. The first has to do with the negative consequences of Eurocentric management styles under African conditions. Older employees were once exposed to oppressive measures by their respective departments, in homelands, in urban areas, in rural areas and on farms. Models that yearn to involve many of these employees might be met with disdain and generally workers would need some form of retraining in new paradigms.

Ubuntu as a philosophy can only be applied at a workplace where employees have gained a level of maturity as professionals. The employees and their management must have understood their role as change agents. Assuming the role of change agents can only be a success when employees know exactly what needs to be done and improved in their organisations.

In his model of five levels of teachers as managers of change, Msila[28] adapts Maxwell's[29] theory above as he draws five levels pertinent in employee change.

i) Transmission level (Level One)

ii) Transcription level (Level Two)

iii) Transmutation level (Level Three)

iv) Transformation level (Level Four)

v) Transcendental level (Level Five)

The attributes of each of the above levels are tabulated as follows:

Table 1.1 Msila's[30] Five Levels of Teacher Change (2002)

Level	Attributes
One *(Accession)*	- Uncritical and will practise what s/he is told - Boss driven - Threatened by change - Might be content with employee isolation
Two *(Accommodating)*	- Understands change but may be apathetic - Simulates the practice of veteran employees - Need to collaborate
Three *(Accepting)*	- Embraces change - Shares the vision of the organisation - Cherishes ongoing employee/people development - Introduction of change within/without the bounds of status quo
Four *(Accentuation)*	- Helps in initiating change - Can be a mentor to others - Co-operates with management - Realises the need for a shared vision and collegiality
Five *(Accomplishment)*	- Manager of change - Commanding respect/asset in a district - Can change others in lower levels - Understands the complexities of change

Msila argues that the first two stages are very basic and are more attributed to novice employees. Many new employees may know nothing about the organisation, may be tentative and may feel unsure about what they need to do in the execution of their duties. They do not want responsibilities as they learn the operations of the organisation.

They may not be ready to understand *ubuntu* principles of working in a team as many want to impress the managers. However, as employees gain experience and the working of the organisation they may be open to models such as *ubuntu*.

Employees who have attained level three upwards will be receptive to *ubuntu* because of their professional development and maturity. It also takes time to move up the ladder of professional maturity and in my research in the past I have found few employees who can be labelled as transcendental employees. Employees in the transcendental stage have achieved much in their careers and are accomplished leaders/managers who sacrifice for others' growth and the success of the organisation.

Two social scientists, Enslin and Horsthemke cite Makgoba, who points out that democracy is not a finished product but an evolutionary one. As pointed out several times above, *ubuntu* cannot be implemented in an organisation that is static, where people are not open to new ideas of fellow employees. Employees need to grow to embrace *ubuntu*; they need to assume 'an evolution of the mind' in order to be ready for it and subsequently embrace *ubuntu* values. Matured leaders/managers will know how to lead the process.

Ubuntu encompasses a process of a cycle of value sharing illustrated in Figure 1.1:

Figure 1.1 displays an environment where *ubuntu* is predominant, where its values surround and anchor the organisation, which in turn enhance the necessary closeness between the followers and the leader. All the elements of the organisation are intertwined and are bound together by an organisation that embraces all.

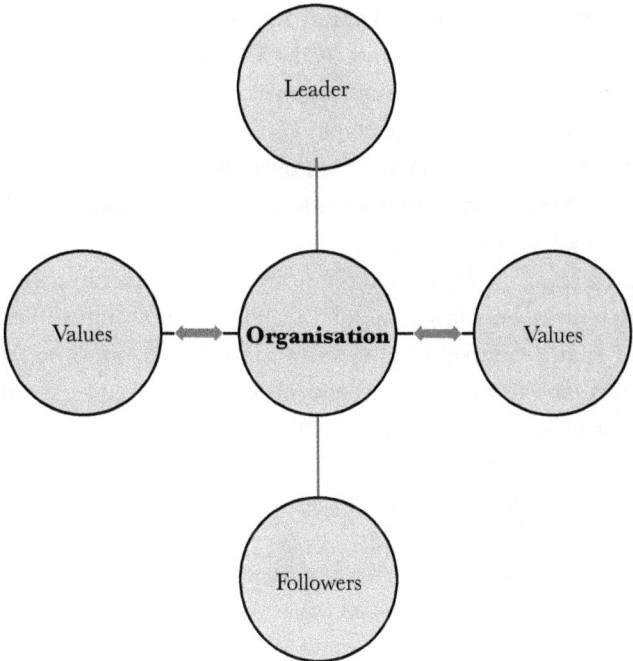

Figure 1.1 Ubuntu cycle of (value-sharing) management

1.5 Ubuntu and need for servant leadership

The above explanation on *ubuntu* shows how organisations need true leaders to lead successful organisations. To be a true African leader one has to be a true servant of the society one lives in. The University of South Africa's principal, Mandla Makhanya[31] refers to servant leadership as an increased service to others, "a holistic approach to work, promoting a sense of community and the sharing of power in decision-making". According to his principal, this is an ideal, a path that his institution wants to follow.

Robert Greenleaf[32], the person who coined this term, *servant leadership*, describes it as a management philosophy that sees the leader as a servant first before s/he can contribute to the well-being of the people and community. The important aspect of servant leadership is that it underscores the importance of serving first before one leads.

Servant leadership defeats the notion of individualism. Committed employees lead with a sense of moral purpose necessary for achieving great organisations. Organisations where there is collaboration, participative or shared leadership have a greater chance of producing employees who practise the common and accepted form of management. Effective managers will try to attain a level of this management that is shared by employees.

Masango[33] writes about how in Africa leadership becomes a function to be shared by all villagers or community members rather than leadership being vested in one person. The African villagers are usually dependent upon the encouragement and support of the leader. S/he was the voice of the village and the villagers represented him/her. The role of the leader was crucial in sustaining the life of the village. Masango[34] aptly writes:

> The whole aim of an effective or life-giving leader is to uplift the villagers/community in such a way that they progress. This will help people to express their own gifts within the village/community. As leaders share their gift of leadership, in return the people will honour them. As they continue to share in African religious ceremonies, which are an essential part of the way of each person, the villagers/community will join the celebration.

As servant leaders, we need to ask ourselves persistent questions. An idle man will never ask the pertinent questions, but a wise human being will constantly ask him- or herself, "What am I doing for others?" "How can I help my neighbour?" Servant leaders are selfless: they focus on other people's needs, and they are happy when others succeed because they are aware that the success of one of the group is a success for everyone. This is the basis of *ubuntu*.

This book is based on the five Ps of *ubuntu*, a theory I have developed over the years when I look at *ubuntu* and its application in workplaces. These five Ps are also very much linked to servant leadership. The five Ps are:

People-centredness: *ubuntu* emphasises the role of the people within the village, the organisation. Without an interest in people, *ubuntu* cannot be realised.

Permeable walls: communication in the village is not restricted and the walls are not opaque. All the members are able to communicate with one another without fear.

Partisanship: one of the most positive factors of the *ubuntu* philosophy is loyalty. People communicate freely and they are made to feel closer to the village.

Progeny: *Ubuntu* leadership promotes collective decision-making. However, under this, effective leadership is respected and the leader is respected.

Production: when the above characterise the village, production is guaranteed. The village prospers when its members enjoy respect, loyalty and good leadership.

The above can be summarised in a table as follows:

Table 1.2 The Five Ps of Ubuntu (Msila, 2002)[35]

Ubuntu – The Five Ps					
People-centredness	Permeable walls	Partisanship	Progeny	Production	

Each of the next five chapters explores each of the Ps and looks at how these can be engendered in the workplace. These five Ps are linked in organisations and might be difficult to discern in well-run organisations.

While the book may refer to those at the helm of organisations as leaders, I know that at times we refer to these as managers. Therefore, although the words are different in meaning, I use these synonymously in this book. Many people still argue, though, that these are very different because people should lead people and manage processes.

This introductory chapter demonstrated the following:

- *Ubuntu* is driven by communal values of interconnectedness.
- *Ubuntu* can revive workplaces.
- *Ubuntu* can be taught.
- *Ubuntu* supports excellence.
- *Ubuntu* supports servant leadership.
- *Ubuntu* encompasses the five Ps in this book.

CHAPTER TWO

PEOPLE-CENTREDNESS

2.1 Introduction

Table 2.1 The Five Ps of ubuntu – **People centredness**

Ubuntu – The Five Ps				
People-centredness	Permeable walls	Partisanship	Progeny	Production

Conscientious leaders will always ensure that their organisations are invitational; that they have the right culture and climate to ensure they thrive, and have committed employees. Unity of purpose and shared vision are among the crucial aspects for an organisation to work. Goals, vision, values and purpose all need to be cultivated in a positive environment.

The major problem that spurs many failures in organisations is that role-players frequently start by focusing outside for problems as they try to explain why things do not work. Usually people forget to look into the culture of the organisation. Change is superficial if it does not look into ways of manipulating culture to make it healthier.

There are times when it is so difficult to change organisational culture, especially when a new manager arrives at a workplace where employees have been for years. Changing culture is always the toughest task – it is even worse when employees have been part of the culture that a manager wants to change. We know how change is usually shunned by people. People like to be comfortable where they are and when no changes are introduced, people are left with a sense of relaxation.

Creating a new corporate culture does not happen haphazardly; it needs to be planned in advance and executed well. Jenn Fusion mentions five crucial steps in engendering a new corporate culture:

Step 1 – Identify and attack the root problems in the existing corporate culture.

Step 2 – Winning people and getting them to be on your side. Let people understand why they need to change.

Step 3 – Start the change management. Employees marvel at managers who literally start the change they want to see. Listening to employees' concerns and continual encouragement is what many employees like to see.

Step 4 – It is important to use each employee according to his/her strength. The environment needs to be exciting for the employees. Interdisciplinary project teams can also bring much difference.

Step 5 – There need to be incentives for change. Wherever possible, employees should get something for embracing and leading change.

Fusion's steps illustrates how involving people may assist in shaping an organisation's direction. A successful corporate culture will be as effective as the people implementing it. There are many other crucial aspects that can be followed in changing corporate culture. Unfortunately, several managers who arrive in new workplaces are reluctant to change cultures as they found them, for various reasons. Among these is the lack of creativity among employees who have internalised boss-driven approaches. These are workers who do not see themselves leading the organisation. Many employees in organisations see the need for change but ironically, they do not think they themselves can be part of that change. They think that it is the manager who is paid to do that.

This chapter focuses on creating people-centred workplaces. In the African village, the focus is on the people at large. The villagers know when any of them fails, the village will also fail. Workplaces should not overlook the importance of instilling a sense of community, a culture of making everybody aware that this is their company and it needs them.

People-centredness is the antithesis of a culture of individuality, greediness and selfishness. An individual who succeeds takes the team along. But setting up people-centred workplaces starts with the culture. The following six stages are crucial in changing culture and making people embrace the organisation as theirs, and can be used in any sequence:

- Set goals
- Convince about change
- Develop leaders
- Improve employee expertise
- Instil a culture
- Support change initiatives.

People used in boss-driven approaches might not like people-centred strategies. This is the reason why this has become so crucial in today's organisation. The above stages attempt to answer a few questions posed by progressive and productive managers. Some of these questions are:

- Which goals do we set for our organisation?
- Why do we need to change our organisation?
- What role do we all have to play?
- How do we improve our expertise?
- Which culture do we want to share?
- How do we support one another?

These are some of the questions that need to be answered by managers who are building people-centred organisations.

2.2 People-centred workplace culture

Ubuntu and its principles based on humanising values should lead to people-centredness. People-centred approaches have the inclination to overcome selfishness, unethical behaviour, corruption and unfairness. When the focus is on everyone in the organisation, employees feel it is their responsibility to uplift the culture therein.

People-centredness in *ubuntu*-driven organisations ensures that employees are content in the workplace and it also enhances team commitment to achieve goals set. People-centredness has the potential of fostering healing in workplaces that are divided by cliques and other debilitating cultures. People-centredness demonstrates clearly to the workers the need for team members to search for collective success in the organisation.

In many organisations, there are people who like to do things their own way, thus acting without considering team goals. However, when people are properly introduced and prepared in an organisation, it is unlikely that there will be people who act outside the team. People in the organisation should see how other members need them for success. When one member flounders, it must be clear that she is failing the entire team.

The introduction of *ubuntu* and people-centredness is not opposed to professionalism and collegial relationships at work. In fact, the strength of *ubuntu*-inspired culture is that it supports moral behaviour or moral culture within an organisation. These are vital for the success of any organisation. Numerous authors have written about the importance of moral, ethics and upright culture in organisations. There will be no following of vision or achievement when workplaces are full of individuals who despise work and are corrupt.

Wharton points out that immoral behaviour persists in organisations because of two factors – a failure to see that the essence of leadership is moral behaviour, and a misunderstanding of how moral actions arise and are inculcated in the workplace. Kirshenbaum also states that morals and values are embodied by character education including respect, responsibility, compassion, self-discipline and loyalty. "Leadership is not about 'technical' (or job) knowledge, it is about followers, those who willingly work their hearts out to get great work done." Moral leadership seeks mutual respect to be engendered within the organisation from top to bottom. Unfortunately managers forget about how moral values are linked to the organisation's success.

I have mentioned the concept of 'community' several times above. This is the crux of solidarity and the major cog in the wheel of *ubuntu* and people-centredness. A workplace as a "community" gives the sense of belonging to team members, the villagers. The village must have water, pastures and everything required for the success of the community. The community members know what happens if one of them spoils the drinking water from the river. They know disaster can happen if they cannot depend upon other villagers. It is also through the community that the villagers express their inner selves.

Moreover, *ubuntu* and people-centredness is about cohesion in the workplace. In a multicultural society such as South Africa, the employees will be able to embrace diversity. People-centredness binds various aspects of the organisation:

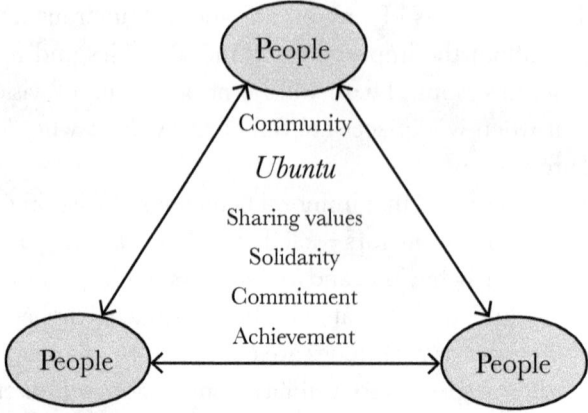

Fig 2.1 People-centredness triangle

One other huge strength of people-centred workplaces bolstered by *ubuntu* is that when people are open, they avail themselves to help others. In many toxic workplaces, competition creates negativity. In search of promotion people tend not to be ready to help others because each wants to be promoted first. We complain in South Africa that pupils straight from school are not ready for the workplace. However, the support the incumbents might get would be far greater if the workplace were people-centred.

2.3 Empowering people — *Ubuntu* African values

In Chapter 1, I stated that if an organisation that emphasises people management could be brought to maturity and be receptive to *ubuntu* people-centred management, it would be more effective. In effective organisations empowered employees will recognise the following:

- Trusting others and learning to coexist
- Employee development of self and others
- Accepting diversity
- Minimising dissension and manipulating culture
- Sharing a vision and fostering solidarity.

Managers need to create other managers within the team. When all employees share management or leadership qualities, it is not difficult to realise the organisation's goals. Employees joining the organisation that respects them, have power to influence the decisions of the organisation. When things are going wrong in the organisation they stand up and state their viewpoints. If one can use the economist and author Albert Hirschman's[36] words, they show voice and loyalty.

In Hirschman's[37] seminal work, *Exit, Voice and Loyalty* the author spells out ways in which customers react to the service they get. Or this may be how employees react to their firms: when there are problems they may react destructively, ie. by neglecting the organisation or exiting.

When employees display neglect, they do not care anymore. They might be in the organisation, but know that they are no longer fruitful. Yet, employees can react constructively through voice or loyalty.

Content employees in a people-centred organisation are likely to show loyalty and voice their concerns when things are not going right. *Ubuntu* fosters this loyalty but it need not be blind loyalty, especially for those employees who are building the organisation. Showing loyalty within a people-centred organisation means that a person shows closeness with the organisation. The organisation may have flaws, but a loyal person will seek to rectify the wrongs through loyal reaction. A person is loyal because she wants to protect the brand of the organisation.

Linked to this is the voice option – a loyal employee will call colleagues to say what is not working and how this needs to be rectified. Voice is crucial in a village and it can be the best way to ensure that things are done right. People-centredness comes with division of responsibilities and this is crucial, because people get to know why they are in the organisation.

People-centredness can be linked to what is referred to as distributed leadership. People-centredness shows elements of distributed leadership. In the people-centredness model, the following are some of the qualities shared with distributed leadership:

- Leadership is not held by a single person
- People have skills and they continually implement these to change the organisation
- Team leadership means responsibilities are shared by all
- Various styles of leadership can be all fused together in people-centred approaches, eg. democratic leadership and authoritarian approaches
- Tasks are fairly known and understood by each of the employees.

It will however, be counterproductive to enforce any strategy on employees. They need to buy into the changes. They need to internalise what the culture of the workplace seeks to achieve. The systems need to ensure that employees own the changes; they should be part of the change process. The people should lead in making the changes with the manager/ leader.

The employee is more likely to be receptive to change initiatives when they are made part of the change process. Whenever change is envisaged, the overall culture of the organisation should be taken into cognisance. But people-centredness is also meaningless if it does not lead to transformational leadership.

2.4 Transformational Leadership

Amongst others, transformational leadership seeks to ensure there is trust and respect in the workplace. Transformational leadership literature explains that transformational leaders are treated with admiration by their fellow employees. Passionate leaders can use the transformational leadership style to bring the necessary positive changes in any organisation, and have the following characteristics:

- They inspire
- They are understanding
- They respect

- They model good actions
- They always boost employee performance.

Managers who use *ubuntu* are likely to have all the above qualities and more. In fact, when a manager embraces *ubuntu*, she also becomes a transformational leader and transformational leaders prepare their employees to be professionally matured. Managers also ensure that with enhanced motivation, their employees learn to embrace moral standards. Employees working with a transformational leader learn to be loyal and are usually intrinsically motivated. They gather energy and a will to succeed and this is why the transformational leader should give the employees enough work, because they want to please and succeed all the time.

The above are all reasons why it is much easier for transformational leaders to have diligent teams. They communicate well and have excellent interpersonal skills. All these are in tandem with the people-centredness that characterises the *ubuntu* philosophy.

The trap that many managers and leaders tend to fall into is not to trust their employees – they don't trust that work will be done well. Employees can see this and will tend not to deliver as a result. With *ubuntu*-inspired models trust is crucial. People-centredness will work well when leaders inspire the followers. The best managers will inspire the employees to be intrinsically motivated to advance the goals of the organisation.

Being transformational starts with the person at the helm of the organisation, and is linked with aspects such as job satisfaction, respect and diligence. In the next chapter we discuss the need for permeable walls, which are also part of transformation leadership.

An unempowered leader cannot have a transformational organisation. Transformation starts with the leader. The leader must live the way he wants to see the organisation. The employees need to see him living the *ubuntu* values that should be running through the entire organisation.

Transformational leaders in organisations:

- **Inspire:** all people know their mission in the organisation.
- **Motivate:** workers need assurance when they are doing right at all times.
- **Influence:** the organisation needs to sense the leader. Their influence needs to be felt in all corners.
- **Support:** people need to be supported at all times. People need to know that aspects such as diligence will be rewarded. People admire a leader who supports them.

All of these need employees who are mentored well. Mentoring is one aspect that successful organisations need. This is discussed at length in Chapter 2, but here we will demonstrate how it is linked to people-centredness.

2.5 Mentoring, *ubuntu* and people-centredness

Any organisation, any leader needs considerate people who will ensure that the organisation thrives as it attains its goals. Organisations want risk takers, thoughtful people who are creative, visionaries and compassionate employees. However, some people do not naturally show these qualities, hence mentoring needs to be part of improving the workplace. When people want to sustain quality and build effective teams, mentoring is the way to go. Employees need to know how to sustain working relationships for the organisation to attain its goals.

Organisations need leaders who are empowered and able to influence their followers. A good people-centred organisation that embraces *ubuntu* will have the following:

- Motivated employees
- Inspiring leaders
- Supportive environment
- Considerate team
- Trusting relationships.

Mentoring – strengthening people-centredness through advice

Mentoring strengthens people-centredness and can also enrich good relations in the workplace. Employees coming from diverse backgrounds may struggle working with one another. Mentoring such employees will go a long way in sustaining good relations.

Mentoring will equip employees on how to use *ubuntu* principles well and mentoring can help in addressing issues such as inequality in organisations. There are various issues of social justice that can be addressed by strong mentoring programmes in workplaces. Unfortunately, in many workplaces people talk about mentoring, but this never becomes a reality. In my previous work and research on mentoring I have noted specific important features of mentoring such as:

- The nature of individual support: how mentors related with their mentees.
- The idea of the "perfect match": what constituted a good mentoring relationship.
- How the mentors and mentees benefited in the mentoring process.
- What created the ideal mentoring relationship.

I have also noted various steps in a successful mentoring relationship and the following diagram illustrates these well:

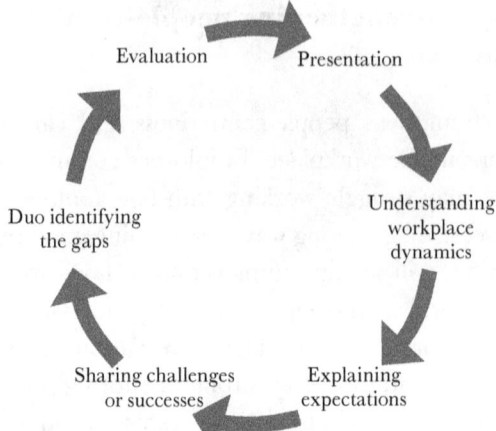

Figure 2.2. Mentoring Cycle

The mentors emphasised the various stages differently as they were informed by their philosophies and the needs of the mentees. The stages can be briefly described as follows:

Presentation

- Mentors explaining their philosophies and experience.
- Mentees describing the nature of their workplaces.

Understanding the organisation dynamics

- Mentees painting pictures of their workplaces.
- Mentors probing.

Explaining expectations

- Mentees' description of their expectations from the relationship.
- Mentors note.

Sharing challenges and successes

- Mentees narrating their story.
- Mentees talking about their philosophies.

Duo identifying gaps

- Interactive sessions as the parties search for answers of how to face challenges or how to make good workplaces better.
- Implementing some suggestions, mainly by the mentee.

Evaluation

- Mentors evaluating the mentoring effects.
- Mentees' assessment of their workplace practice.

The success of all these stages is dependent on the mutual trust between the mentor and mentee. From the beginning where the mentee presents facets of his/her organisation, some rapport needs to be established, otherwise honest reflection will not happen and the process of mentoring will be a farce, because mentees will not share all. Therefore working together well is likely to lead to effective mentorship.

When the mentor and mentees open up and share their experiences, growth happens. One mentee in one of my studies pointed out that reflecting on their practice with the mentor is "the most enriching experience of the mentoring encounter". In this way mentoring leads to transformational learning as mentees tend to lead the discussions with mentors showing elements of self-development and self-criticism.

Ubuntu-driven organisations need these mentoring processes because they enhance even the process of reflection. Mentoring also helps because it helps people understand themselves better. There is no way that people can work well with others when they do not understand themselves.

Good mentoring builds organisations. Yet organisations should ensure that they look at some of the potential challenges in mentoring programmes:

Experience and choosing the right mentor

One major challenge in the above was the challenge of choosing effective mentors. Until one sees the mentor-mentee experience it is difficult to predict whether the relationship would yield results. In the case studies some participants listed the qualities of good mentors. All organisations should ensure that mentors and mentorship initiatives will be supported continuously. Unprepared mentors can never guide teachers to be diligent practitioners that they need to be. The Wallace Foundation (2007)[38] underscores the flaw of not holding mentors accountable and not training them seriously. Another challenge though are the costs that a mentorship programme can amount to.

Costs and mentoring programmes

Effective mentoring strategies can cost companies because good mentoring can be such a demanding process that needs the commitment of both the mentor and the mentee. Strategic organisations will set aside special budget for meaningful mentoring as they ensure that mentors are also constantly trained to know the demands of the 21st century organisation. Mentoring programmes cannot be sustained without this training.

Investing in mentoring for organisations is to enable the organisation to achieve its set goals and build better employees who are confident. People frequently ask whether mentoring programmes are worth the money spent. Good mentoring programmes ensure that practice is improved and employee turnover is reduced. In fact, much research has shown that mentoring may force the organisations to use more money, but this can have huge benefits for the organisations:

- *Diversity management* – employees will be able to work in diverse environments.
- *Improved organisational culture* – employees need to learn to create and sustain a working culture for their organisation.
- *Developing change managers* – all employees need to be effective change managers to drive their organisation forward.
- *Identification of employees' talents* – mentoring helps in discovering the employees' strengths.
- *Developing professionally matured employees* – a philosophy such as *ubuntu* may need employees to be mentored to understand and engender a sense of purpose in the organisation.

Both the mentors and mentees benefit from the mentoring process as they constantly become aware of themselves.

Culture as a potential obstacle to mentoring

In multicultural societies, cultures can be a hindrance to effective mentoring. Understanding issues of diversity is very important for all mentors in a culturally diverse society. Ethnocentrism will kill the mentoring relationship. Mentors need to understand the cultural dynamics at play when they are engaged in a mentoring relationship with those from different cultural backgrounds. Used well, different cultures will enrich the mentor-mentee relationships; this is the paradox of different cultures. In the process of learning from other cultures, mentees can be prepared for diverse working environments. In fact, cultural difference should be used to enhance the mentoring experience.

Effective mentors will be change agents who understand cultures and possess certain necessary qualities. Villani[39] states that a good mentor has the following qualities:

- positively disposed to serve colleagues' growth
- culturally competent and proficient

- secure enough to value the different and evolving leadership styles of new managers
- committed to promoting a new principal's reflection
- generous and willing to share resources and ideas
- lifelong learners
- an effective communicator.

All the above qualities will help the mentor develop mentees. However, mentors will not have these without understanding the cultures of the mentees. Linked to the element of culture as an obstacle is history affecting the mentees.

History as hindrance to mentoring

South African education has a unique history considering that the education of different racial and sometimes tribal groups varied during apartheid days. When mentors do not understand the history of the mentees, this can create problems. Mentees who come from environments where certain practices have been internalised (even when not regarded acceptable) might not readily understand the mentor's role and may even be apathetic to the intervention. It is then crucial to understand the history affecting what informs the practices of mentees.

Like other authors cited above, Jazzar and Algozzine[40] emphasise the need to use effective criteria in selecting mentors, and the understanding of history should be among these. They say these criteria should include communication skills, knowledge of politics, positive attitude and attributes, professional competence and trustworthiness.

Both leaders and the general employees will gain from the mentoring processes in *ubuntu* driven organisations. New leaders in organisations should ensure that there are always plans for mentoring in their organisations. Mentoring can be the difference between motivated and unmotivated employees, between team players and selfish individuals. Mentoring shows direction and enhances the shared vision that I briefly discuss in the next subsection.

2.6 Shared vision

People-oriented leadership is about leaders who continually inspire the employees in their organisations to share a common vision. People-centred organisations are successful because employees move towards the attainment of one vision. Leaders will know that organisations belong to people and collective decisions will ensure that employees craft their own vision. Shared vision implies that:

- Employees have found common ground
- They have the interest of the organisation at heart
- They are goal-directed
- They are moving towards a common destination.

Leaders who have great visions should communicate these and share with employees. Even a great vision can fail if employees do not own it. Intelligent leaders will always discuss their vision with their team. They have their employees as critical others who will explore the vision as it is discussed.

This will be easy in transparent and honest organisations. Inspirational leaders will magnify the goal, open up the organisation for participation; show the need for moving toward a certain direction and build hope in the organisation. Showing employees a shared vision is a project of inspirational leaders. Inspirational leaders also know that in *ubuntu*-inspired organisations, a shared vision:

- Begins with a personal vision
- Can prosper when trust is displayed to employees
- Is part of solidarity
- Accommodates dissent and that diverse opinions enhance the organisation
- Advances *ubuntu* ideals.

All these show that the organisation is not about the leader only. The organisation is about the people.

2.7 The organisation is about us, not you

This chapter has shown that organisation is not only about those in leadership positions. Some leaders have a tendency to own achievements, thinking that the organisation's success can only be attributed to their leadership. Leaders who do this, though, will not be able to halt staff turnover of good members of staff. People in any workplace like to be acknowledged.

Wise leaders will ensure that they let their employees share the laurels. When they do this it is easy for employees to own failures as well as try and find solutions to the problems experienced by the organisations. Again, these are crucial issues for *ubuntu*-driven organisations. This book stresses this aspect throughout. *Ubuntu* principles demonstrate that there is no organisation that is about its leadership only. Leadership is part of a team and all good leaders will know that "the organisation is not about me". All employees treasure the following:

- Being included in making collective decisions
- Being complemented when things go well
- Being consulted in times of change
- Being supported when support is needed
- Being taken seriously.

When leaders follow these they are likely to have successful employees who cherish the dreams of the organisation. A good leader will be secure in his /her position knowing fully that solidarity is crucial in the organisation. Effective leaders like and support people oriented organisation because:

- Others' strong points are not seen as a threat
- Great teams make grand organisations

- Survival of the organisation needs more than the leader
- The control of the organisation needs working teams
- Diversity in teams can be used as the organisation's strength
- Collectivity encourages growth.

Therefore, if there are any words that successful leaders always need to think about they are: **THE ORGANISATION IS NOT ABOUT THEM.**

This chapter demonstrated the following:

- There is always a need to create a culture that would be receptive to people-centredness.
- Effective leaders will empower people as they inculcate *ubuntu* values for people-centredness.
- People-centredness is amenable to transformational leadership.
- Mentoring will support *ubuntu* and people-centredness.
- Creating a learning organisation may lead to people-centredness.
- Organisation is about us, not you alone!

CHAPTER THREE

PERMEABLE WALLS

3.1 Introduction

Table 3.1 The Five Ps of ubuntu – Permeable walls

Ubuntu requires full participation of all the employees in the organisation and this cannot happen when there is no communication. A drum would be sounded in the middle of the village to call all the villagers and to announce important developments. But even after this big meeting, the villagers would communicate with one another about all the important factors in the village.

But people cannot communicate when the conditions are not right. The community needs to reinforce the village connectedness through effective communication. Some of the qualities discussed in the previous chapters such as trust, openness, solidarity and respect enhance effective communication in an organisation. In the village, this communication helps and ensures that the villagers are aware of what the community needs to do at all times. It is effective communication that enables people to understand the collective roles in the organisation.

Proper communication in organisations is also important for co-ordination, frequent explanations about rituals of the organisation and ensuring that there is a coherent plan in the community. Communication makes sure that the community is always in a well co-ordinated environment that is not haphazard and uncertain. Communication is not only crucial for the organisation's internal operations; it is effective co-ordination that sells the organisation to the outside world. Communication is the only way that stakeholders and role players will know what the organisation is doing.

Organisations in Africa and the world are largely diverse today because people come from various cultural backgrounds. We should ensure that communication is not a barrier amongst team members. Organisations need to inculcate a culture within an organisation that symbolically embodies the rules of communication. Intercultural communication can create conscious and unconscious problems within the organisation. There are a number of aspects that can kill the spirit of the team in organisations. These are some of the examples:

- Ethnocentrism
- Language differences
- Tribalism
- Xenophobia
- Hierarchical positions
- Prejudices

An *ubuntu* worldview addresses each of these. In fact, in the world of *ubuntu*, which espouses among other things solidarity, these do not exist. *Ubuntu* addresses these ills because it is based on building a community. The reality, though, is that workplaces have become rife with some of these ills. These are bred by a society that is shifting from humanitarian values.

Effective communication will conquer these ills. This chapter explores ways in which employees in the workplace can combat poor communication. It illustrates how we can use *ubuntu* to construct walls that are permeable. Workplaces will have walls, but they need not be impenetrable. Today's organisations have various forms of communication at their disposal and these include social media such as Twitter, Facebook, e-mail and mobile phones. All of these can be used to improve communication in organisations.

In organisations communication can either be external or internal. External communication is used to communicate with stakeholders outside the organisation while internal communication is for people within the organisation.

Furthermore, communication can adopt various directions. In the old top-down organisations, communication used to be in one direction from management to subordinates. It happens sometimes that communication can be upward, from employees to management or horizontal (peer-to-peer). *Ubuntu* uses communication that is diagonal or multi-directional, where various modes may be used to communicate. In fact, *ubuntu* maintains that communication must be a collective effort as all members have to take part. What characterises *ubuntu* communication is its open nature or transparency.

3.2 Openness and honesty: Supporting relationships

In the community of the company, communication has to be undergirded by the values of openness. Communication in an *ubuntu*-inspired organisation is not only about ensuring full participation of community members but also about ensuring that relationships are supported by the spirit of collegiality. Effective communication ensures that the following are sustained:

- Solidarity is communicated
- Talk constantly about the vision
- Cement the organisation's relationships
- Share ideas around the issues of improving the community
- Verbalise the efforts of others as the goals of the organisation are planned.

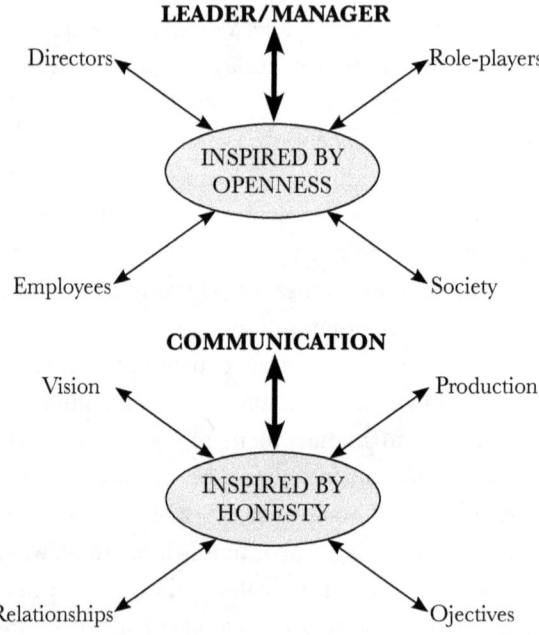

Figure 3.1 Communication Web

The above figure shows how permeable walls of *ubuntu* stand on openness and honesty. A good leader will lead effective communication and ensure that community members and the organisation's directors witness transparency. If the organisation is failing it cannot achieve any profits and this has to be communicated well.

The community is unlikely to know what is right and what is wrong when there is a lack of openness. An organisation that is open and transparent will have members who are able to be loyal or voice their opinions when they feel it needs to be improved.

- The directors need to know what is happening – what needs to be improved – and it is crucial *how* this is communicated.
- The employees cannot lead the organisation to success unless information is communicated well to them. Organisations sometimes fail because employees are made to feel like outsiders.
- There are many role players who have vested interests in the organisation. They also need to know what a company stands for. They need to know what is in it for them.
- The general society or larger community also needs to understand what the organisation stands for. Some organisations might be producing computers but are also champions for peace education, social justice and nutrition. But all this needs to be communicated so that communities know what the organisation is all about.

Communication also needs to be inspired by honesty when tackling aspects such as vision and relationships. Organisations should be able to agree when they divert from their actual objectives. The latter helps in building a strong organisation.

It is difficult to think of *ubuntu* without thinking about effective communication. Communication is the engine in the functioning of the *ubuntu* system. Nothing can be achieved in an organisation without strong and meaningful communication. Great plans, august strategies, all will flounder when these ideas cannot be fed well to various parts of the organisation. *Ubuntu*'s communication needs to feed through the entire organisation to sustain it. Therefore, bad leaders can kill grand plans through a lack of communication. The following figure 3.2 illustrates the crucial nature of communication.

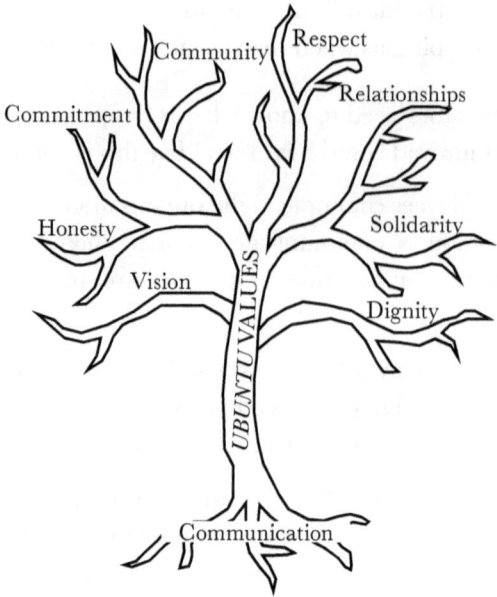

Figure 3.2 *Ubuntu values tree*

There are many other values that can be added to the above branches. All these are fed by the roots of effective communication. Communication is pivotal to sharing the goals or the destination where the organisation should go. Effective communication cannot be one-sided. We need permeable walls so that information can come from both sides. Because *ubuntu* is based on respect and dignity, this means that all the members of the community should have a say. When a leader communicates ideas s/he should wait for feedback and discussion.

Scott and Mitchell[41] mention four functions of communication:

All of these are essential for the progress in organisations and we have already seen how they apply in working organisations. Communication also helps in times of uncertainty when employees are not sure about change and job security. Therefore, apart from helping employees to understand policies and organisational tasks, communication can avert disappointment in the workplace.

3.3 Barriers of communication

Among the barriers mentioned by Crafford[42] are filtering, selective perception and information overload. Crafford[43] presents these as a number of interpersonal and intrapersonal barriers in addition to those mentioned above.

3.3.1 Filtering

In large corporations a sender may manipulate information so that it can be perceived in a favourable light by the receiver.

3.3.2 Selective perception

People may not see reality; instead they may interpret what they see and call it reality.

3.3.3 Information overload

When people have more information than they can sort out, they tend to select, ignore, or forget.

3.3.4 Defensiveness

Sometimes people may feel as if they are threatened and they become defensive as they retaliate using, for example, sarcasm.

3.3.5 Language

One of the major challenges in organisations is the use of different languages. People may interpret communication differently when it is communicated in a third or fourth language. In an *ubuntu* environment this is one area that needs to be addressed because the community cannot survive when the members cannot understand each other. There are a number of ways that managers may explore to fight barriers and improve their communication skills.

Crafford[44] suggests useful ways that leaders can use to improve their communication:

1. **Use multiple channels** – when more than one channel is used, clarity is improved and more people are likely to receive and understand the message.

2. **Tailor the message for the audience** – jargon used with one section of the company may be confusing to others who are not specialists in a particular area.

3. **Empathise with others** – when speaking it is crucial for people to empathise with the listeners. They need to be sensitive to their needs.

4. **When dealing with change, face-to-face communication is important** – when information is threatening and ambiguous it is better to convey messages face-to-face. A lot of information can be transmitted during face-to-face communication.

5. **Practice active listening** – listening is crucial in communication. Active listening ensures that the other person is given time to say what they need to say. This is very important in an attempt to understand them.

6. **Match your words and actions** – people should not be confused; the non-verbal should be equal to the verbal. When managers are inconsistent they lose the respect of their colleagues.

7. **Use the grapevine** – the grapevine cannot be ignored, therefore management can use the grapevine to improve formal communication. In a village there will always be a grapevine; it is not necessarily bad and can be used by clever managers.

3.4 Direction of the organisation: Communication and *ubuntu*

The idea of *ubuntu* is a challenge to those used to working alone. Leaders working in *ubuntu*-driven organisations learn the idea of community when it comes to communication. Leaders in these organisations listen as communities (the people) speak.

Leaders need to be conscious as to how they promote communities that are able to communicate the aspirations of the organisations as well as their own ideas well. It is the spirit of *ubuntu* and effective communication that lead to solidarity, collaboration and consensus. Employees may differ in discussions, but at the end consensus will be reached because all seek to achieve community goals bigger than individuals. Effective communication defies obstacles as people share ideas. The critical aspect in organisations is that communication in an *ubuntu* environment has built-in strategies to combat distrust and conflicts.

> This chapter demonstrated the following:
>
> - *Ubuntu* requires all people to perform well.
> - Co-ordination will not happen without effective communication.
> - Leaders should be careful of aspects that can kill the team spirit in organisations.
> - Openness and honesty supports good communication.
> - Leaders should avoid barriers to effective communication.
> - *Ubuntu* implies good communication.

CHAPTER FOUR

PARTISANSHIP

4.1 Introduction

Table 4.1 The Five Ps of ubuntu – Partisanship

Loyalty to the village is one aspect I highlighted several times in the previous chapters. Earlier I cited the work of Hirschman's[45] *Exit, Voice and Loyalty* where Hirschman[46] writes about how employees react to organisations when they are satisfied or discontent.

People become loyal when they are satisfied with their organisation, and loyalty will be shown by people who witness trust, solidarity and progress in an organisation. They will be

47

proud of their association with the organisation. People appreciate and respect dignity shown in the organisation.

In any workplace job satisfaction is important, so people will generally leave an organisation when they are not satisfied.

Partisanship is interested in the loyalty of the employees. The employees who want their organisation to succeed will be loyal at all times and again, it takes a good leader to foster partisanship among followers in an *ubuntu*-driven organisation.

Hirschman's[47] work spells out ways in which employees or members of an organisation can behave when their organisation does not please them. When they see quality dwindling, they can either exit (withdraw their services) or they can exercise voice (trying to improve relationship) in various ways including grievance procedures or proposals for change. The third option is loyalty.

Miller[48] summarises how employees can express dissatisfaction:

> **Exit:** behaviour directed towards leaving the organisation, including looking for a new position, as well resigning.
>
> **Voice:** actively and constructively attempting to improve conditions, including suggesting improvements, discussing problems with supervisors and some forms of union activity.
>
> **Loyalty:** passively but optimistically waiting for conditions to improve, including speaking up for the organisation in the face of external criticism and trusting the organisation and its management to "do the right thing".
>
> **Neglect:** passively allowing conditions to worsen, including chronic absenteeism or lateness, reduced effort and increased error rate.

Dowding et al.[49] refer to the above as the EVLN model. These authors also look at the costs of voice and exits:

> Exiting from one product to another when both are next to another on a supermarket shelf is costless, whereas complaining about the product may be very inconvenient. In another context, exiting is very costly. Switching jobs for example or moving house. Voice is often more costly than exit with less assured results. (Dowding *et al.* [50])

Employees can exercise any of these options when reacting to waning quality in an organisation. Whitford and Lee[51] found that satisfaction with the organisation minimises the likelihood of employees stating their intention to leave for all exit options (exit/voice/loyalty).

Dowding *et al.* also highlight the importance of empowering public sector employees. "Empowering public employees through increasing voice makes them perceive that they have greater discretion and decide to opt into or stay in employment in the public sector"[52]. When public sector employees have a belief that they have a voice, they can halt their mobility.

Farrell and Rusbult[53] use the EVLN model by showing how it enhances our understanding of organisational behaviour in several ways. They define exit, voice, loyalty and neglect in terms of two dimensions, namely, constructive versus destructiveness, as well as activity versus passivity. People who are satisfied with their jobs will be constructive using voice and loyalty. However, employees who are dissatisfied are likely to react destructively through neglect or exit.

Farrell and Rusbult[54] use the following diagram to illustrate the EVLN model:

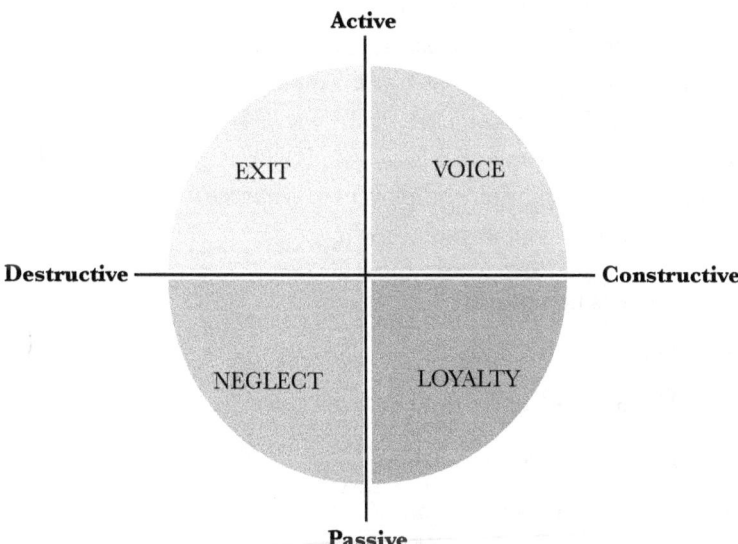

Fig 4.1 A typology of responses to job dissatisfaction (Farrell & Rusbult 1992:203)[55]

In the above figure 4.1, Farrell and Rusbult[56] demonstrate the application of Hirschman's[57] exit options. At various points in their lives many workers who are frustrated in their organisations may experience one or several of these options.

Instilling loyalty among employees is crucial for productivity. When an employee is loyal s/he identifies with the organisation. When an employee goes to work he says, I am going to my company". It is their village, their community they are going to and they say that with pride. Loyalty is about intense identification. The organisation, the people, the successes and the failures are part of an employee.

From the first day employees start at a workplace there needs to be a will to instil the values of loyalty. Due to the economic situation of today one may find that people, especially the younger generation, tend to be less loyal to their workplaces. I have talked to various teaching employees over the years and found that generally six out of 10 would jump ship if they could find opportunities anywhere else. This is an exit option that many would prefer rather than stick within the organisation, and in such circumstances managers should try and instil the much needed sense of loyalty among employees.

Leaders who practise *ubuntu* should not have many challenges in inspiring employees to be loyal. Employees who see loyalty and are respected, are more likely to be loyal. Loyalty starts with the company's management. *Ubuntu* values when followed will make it easy for leaders to inspire employees to embrace loyalty. Employees will not be loyal in a workplace where:

- There is no respect
- There is uncertainty
- There are no opportunities
- There is employee isolation
- There is no communication.

Money is what all employees would like to have because it gives them and their families a better life. However, even with money, employees also want to be happy. Employees may not really enjoy their money and benefits when they find that they do not belong. Loyalty means belonging and being committed to an organisation.

For management it is difficult to work with employees who are not loyal. Employees who are not loyal:

- Do not care about company goals (assuming they even know them)

- Do not care what happens to fellow employees, when they themselves are safe

- Do not care of opportunities within the company because they are to retire soon or are looking elsewhere for a position

- Do not care in changing the workplace for the better – it is none of their business!

There is no work place that can be built if its foundations have workers with these values. Loyalty means focus and owning responsibilities as you aspire for success. In *ubuntu*-driven organisations this loyalty should be a burden of the entire community. It is difficult to have loyalty in a workplace where there is no solidarity, where there are cliques and where there are no warm relationships. Everyone wins when employees are loyal, so it is important to develop loyalty built on good values.

4.2 Building loyalty through organisational values

This book has generally discussed much about using culture and values in organisations. Diligent and committed employees can be created by effective leaders, through the instilling of effective values. Yet any organisation needs to start with culture before it can have diligent employees who are loyal to the organisation.

When it is applied as it should be, *ubuntu* can enable any organisation to thrive. Various examples have been illustrated already. The following are elements that can also enable the leader to create loyal employees:

- Being a Cultivator
- Sharing a Calabash of ideas
- Promoting Collegiality (Camaraderie)
- Ploughing Commitment.

4.2.1 Being a Cultivator

A cultivator wants to see his/her seeds growing well so that when it is time to reap, all is in good order. In the village during the sowing season, when men and women go to the fields, they do not expect to see results immediately. It may take months before they can reap from what they have sown.

The leader needs to be the cultivator in the organisation, working with employees to cultivate the seeds they want for their organisation. It is also critical that the cultivator sows what he would like to reap. The fields need to be the reflection of the leader.

Employees will be loyal to the organisation when they see that the cultivator plants with the success of the community – the organisation – in mind. What the cultivator reaps later s/he must be able to share with others, because it is good. The employees would like an organisation that has them in mind when planning is done.

Therefore, effective leaders will be strategic thinkers who are cultivators!

4.2.2 Sharing a Calabash

In any African community there is a time when the community sits down around a big fire and a calabash of beer is shared around. Everyone has his/her turn to sip from the calabash. This brings the community together. It can be a village feast, maybe a wedding or maybe a sacrifice to the ancestors. This can be a time of reflection for the villagers where they may plan their future as they reflect on the past. Hunters, for example, may meet around this fire to discuss their next adventure. They may share what they need to do to ensnare the lion that keeps on devouring their cattle.

Effective leaders will make their employees comfortable by symbolically moving around the calabash, sharing ideas to build the organisation. When people sit with others to share the calabash, they feel important because they also influence the future of the organisation. They feel equal to all other members, hence their loyalty is enhanced. Effective managers will continually share ideas in the organisation and share with colleagues to criticise.

Therefore, creative leaders will share ideas as they ensure that all employees drink from the same calabash!

4.2.3 Promoting Collegiality (Camaraderie)

When employees feel the support of their colleagues, they love the workplace and look forward at going to work. Camaraderie in the workplace is good for enhancing professionalism, identification and being one of the team members. Collegiality helps people to feel that they belong.

Big organisations engender collegiality because they know it can sustain organisations as it builds trust and loyalty among employees. Employees bound together by collegiality learn from one another and are not afraid to criticise one another. The criticism, though, is not personal and is for the advancement of the organisation.

Wise leaders build collegiality to sustain their organisations and enhance loyalty!

Numerous people maintain that when organisations have employee loyalty it is likely that they will also have client loyalty. Leaders may be able to tell when they have loyal employees. Not only are these employees motivated but they display certain attributes that can be engendered. Loyal employees illustrate the values of the *ubuntu*-driven organisation. Below I focus on some of the qualities that are displayed by loyal employees.

4.2.4 Ploughing commitment

This book has several times highlighted the need for loyalty and commitment. Organisational performance is largely dependent upon employee commitment. There is much research that illustrates how crucial it is for managers who want productivity to inculcate commitment.

When employees have commitment they demonstrate:

- Shared vision
- Goal directedness
- Organisational responsibility
- Values-driven performance.

Work commitment strengthens the community ethic as employees work towards the same goal. Effective managers will facilitate commitment by preparing a conducive climate. Employees cannot be forced to be committed, but managers should create conditions for employees to have reasons as to why they need to be committed. Commitment may go hand in glove with satisfaction. In fact, it is satisfied employees who will be committed to their organisation.

The idea of associating with a community in the workplace when using *ubuntu* shows how *ubuntu* generates commitment. Commitment is an ingredient of survival in the village/organisation. It is difficult to think of *ubuntu* without thinking about commitment. The *ubuntu* culture breaks individualism as it promotes teams and the work ethic.

4.3 Qualities displayed by loyal employees

i) They **criticise** for the general good of the group. By criticism they do not wish to be disrespectful to anybody, but rather to ensure that the organisation becomes successful. Loyal members do say it to the leader when they feel he is not on the right track. They speak with respect, but they are honest. These are the only ways that organisations can grow.

ii) Loyal members are interested in **listening** and **hearing** what other people say. This is the way to build organisations to listen to others and commit to their aspirations. Loyal members are usually employees who have some leadership qualities. They know how to talk to colleagues to preach the idea of collective responsibility.

iii) Loyal employees **fight** for the success of the organisation. They do not rest until they are certain that their organisation is on the path to success. Loyal employees do not easily give up, for they believe there is always hope that the organisation will succeed if all the people should stand together.

iv) Loyal employees **follow** their leader even in trying times. Frequently, when things do not go right members may want to abandon the leader's ship, especially when all are critical of the leader. Loyal employees know that at times the vision may not be in sight as the leader tries to work on old internalised cultures. Loyal employees will work on old internalised cultures. Loyal employees will work with the leader as they try to find the right paths.

v) They are **honest** about what they can or cannot do in an organisation. Loyal members are always open about their ability, hence it is easy for the leader to see the training gaps required. A loyal employee does not overstate what s/he can do because s/he understands the crucial nature of this in the success of the organisation.

vi) Loyal employees take it upon themselves to **empower** others. When they see the inadequacies in others, loyal employees try and work towards helping others. They carefully and warmly negotiate their way through without imposing themselves. They do this because it is for the common good of all in the organisation.

These are all important but cannot be attained when a leader is not loyal to the organisation.

4.4 Leader/manager loyalty — I am because of this community

When people talk of loyalty it is usually employees that we think about, and rarely do we think of leaders. In many cases, unfortunately, management can be bureaucratic and uncaring. *Ubuntu*-driven organisations are about using emotion as part of the bigger picture of the organisation or community.

Effective leaders can enable employees to be loyal. An uncaring leader can hardly make the employees loyal. Employees see it when leaders are not committed to the organisation. This book talks about the need for the leaders to be matured in order to lead change. Loyal members of an organisation become change agents. Organisations with members who are not loyal are stagnant and unfriendly. Loyalty enhances a number of things and among these are relationships, trust, belief and production.

Carol Kinsey Goman[58] points out that loyalty has two dimensions:

i. The internal or emotional level. Goman[59] points out that loyalty is a feeling of bonding, mutuality, affiliation or trust. Furthermore, loyalty manifests itself as caring and concern for other people.

ii. External or behavioural aspect. We can look at people's behaviour to see their loyalty. People will show certain actions towards the organisation as well as other employees to exhibit their loyalty.

What I am showing in this book is that loyalty can be engendered through the right values. Many workplaces have a high staff turnover because there are no values that underscore loyalty. Building a loyal workforce should always be chief in the agenda of ambitious leaders – but of course as stated above, loyalty begins with those at the helm.

It is great for the organisation to have loyal members, but they need to be strong employees. Nothing is worse for an organisation than weak, loyal employees. Weak employees are scared to oppose authority; they simply do things to please others even when they do not agree with those decisions.

Strong employees, however, are loyal because loyalty is beneficial to themselves and others; the community or the organisation. *Ubuntu* does not want people to live in fear – it needs to be based on respect. As soon as people are loyal because they fear, then it cannot be *ubuntu* because *ubuntu* does not promote negative values such as fear. Fear, suspicion, disrespect, cruelty, and nepotism are some of the negative values in workplaces that can lead to high staff turnover as well as disloyalty.

Leaders and managers who are loyal and preach loyalty display the following qualities:

- Commitment
- Affection
- Reward
- Empathy.

4.4.1 Committed

These leaders are committed and caring and they want other members to have these qualities too. No leader can be loyal without showing some commitment to the organisation. In fact, *ubuntu* is about commitment. People are loyal to the village, the community or the organisation because they are committed.

4.4.2 Affectionate

Collegiality can be practised within a highly affective workplace. *Ubuntu* supports relationships. Employees can be loyal to the organisation because they are respected, valued and appreciated. People-centredness discussed in Chapter 2 illustrates the role affectionate leadership/ management plays in an organisation. An affectionate leader loves working with his/her employees.

4.4.3 Rewarding

There is nothing that repels people more from the organisation than people who are not rewarded for the good they do. Leaders who reward their employees are likely to get loyal employees. Rewards are not about money only. Complimenting employees, small gifts for good work done, and trophies are all good when fairly distributed.

When money and gifts are involved, though, it is important for the company to be transparent. People should know the procedures followed and this has to be achieved through collective decision-making. Rewarding employees can achieve a number of things:

- Strengthens good practices
- Change attitudes for the better
- Increase production
- Create positive competition.

4.4.4 Empathy

The feeling or thinking in *ubuntu models* is enhanced by empathy. In *ubuntu*-driven communities the people feel with their fellow human beings. Leaders who are sincere and feel with their employees will have a loyal workforce.

In pursuit of production and success, leaders frequently ignore empathy. The lack thereof may be interpreted in several ways by employees.

4.5 Shared moral values and loyalty

The challenge leaders have in organisations is to ensure that employees share moral values. The challenge of any new leader is to try and ensure that people have certain values to share, especially when the culture in an organisation makes it unworkable.

When there is no positive culture in an organisation there is no positive identity that defines the organisation. When employees share moral values they become strong as a team and show allegiance to the vision of the organisation. People need to share allegiance: it makes them loyal.

Shared moral values have a huge impact on ethics and norms. Smart and conscientious managers are aware that ethical leadership starts with sharing of values; *ubuntu* values do embrace shared moral values. The in-group respect that one finds in the organisations ensures that people relate deeply with one another.

The diagram below illustrates how loyalty can be engendered in organisations. This cannot be allowed to happen on its own in today's organisations and needs to be planned well:

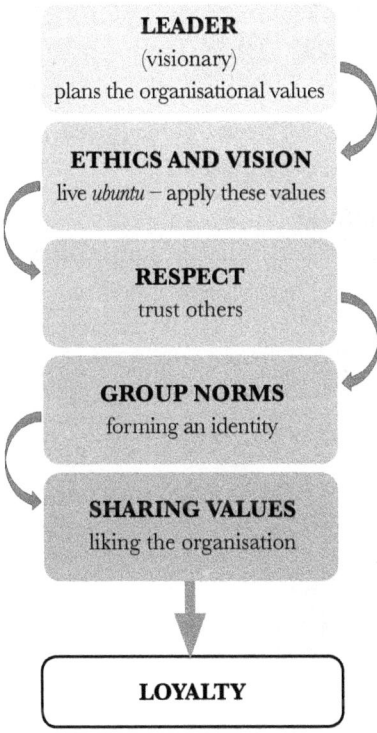

Figure 4.2 Engendering loyalty

Again, wise leaders will work to see that members of the organisations are loyal, because all organisations want to succeed. The above diagram can have many other permutations, but what is crucial is that the people at the helm should drive the belief in organisational values. Sharing moral values should be ingrained in the employees' belief system.

> This chapter highlighted the following:
>
> - The more loyal employees are to the organisation, the stronger the organisation.
> - Loyalty shows that employees have trust in the organisation.
> - Loyal employees may strengthen the organisation by exercising the voice option.
> - There is always a need to engender shared moral values and loyalty in organisations.
> - Loyalty starts with the manager/leader.

CHAPTER FIVE

PROGENY

5.1 Introduction

Table 5.1 The Five Ps of ubuntu – **Progeny**

Progeny deals with collective decision-making. Both leaders and their followers make decisions, which means that their collective decision-making becomes part of the posterity of the organisation. This may change from time to time but each generation of workers will have and own its collective decisions.

Ubuntu as a philosophy realises the need of a community or a village or an organisation to survive. When decisions are made, people think of one another in an organisation.

Other authors have aligned collective decision-making to human rights and political power. Metz[60] argues:

> One can fairly sum up these rights by saying that citizens are entitled to an equal opportunity to influence political outcomes. Now, if what is special about us is, in part, our ability to identify with others or to share a way of life, then that is going to require sharing political power. And supposing we are equally special by virtue of having the requisite capacity to share a way of life, that means according people the equal ability to influence collective decision-making.

All the members of the organisation should be treated equally as they influence decision-making. Collective decision-making largely makes use of consensus in arriving at decisions. The challenge of the leader today is ensuring that everyone becomes loyal to some decisions.

Organisations are very diverse in their make-up. One will find Muslims, Christians, traditional religious people, whites, blacks, gays and heterosexuals. The challenge here is to try and reach a consensus as people adopt collective decision-making. Consensus requires loyalty and conformity to some idea or some goals. There is no way that a group can reach consensus without solidarity and common goals.

The latter is crucial for reinforcing relationships and ensuring that productivity is positively affected. Strategic planning needs to be sensitive and respond to *ubuntu* values.

In some workplaces, those who are not fluent in the dominant language used tend to be withdrawn and keep to themselves. Generally in organisations, people who do not have the social capital will tend to sit at the back and keep quiet. *Ubuntu*'s collective decision-making is opposed to this. Everyone needs to participate in group discussions and collective decision-making.

It is also important for the management team to consult from the guard at the gate to the CEO of the company. *Ubuntu* breaks down the obstacles usually set between management and ordinary workers on the shop floor. We have seen in the previous chapters how *ubuntu* is intent on building relationships and strengthening organisational values. Leaders and managers using *ubuntu* values for decision-making have the following qualities:

- *Valuing* employees
- *Appreciating* their input
- *Listening* intently to all suggestions
- *Understanding* what people say
- *Empathising* with all employees.

All five aspects are a cornerstone in collective decision-making. Effective leaders/ managers are those who have certain qualities. These are people who can put aside their selfish needs to take care of the organisation and the people.

In the village, there are the kinship ties that enable the villagers to survive. Kinship in the workplace is important in that:

- it enhances teamwork
- it magnifies trust
- people feel reassured
- implementing the decisions become easy.

Even African folktales usually want to spread these aspects because for centuries social mores that arouse unity were based on these. Many stories from all over Africa stress the importance of togetherness.

This chapter explores progeny – the manner in which the manager/ leader creates a generation of decision-makers in the workplace. This ensures that everyone in the company thinks. In many companies, many who work in the shop floor may not bother to think about company goals because the "big meeting's in the boardroom exclude them. They know that their ideas do not matter when people talk about ways to accomplish the company's vision.

This chapter clarifies progeny under the following topics:

- Strengthening relationships and solidarity
- Sharing power
- Mutual understanding
- Building better teams
- Using humanness to chase a vision.

These are all interlinked and they encapsulate the basic tenets of *ubuntu* connected to collective decision-making.

5.2 Strengthening relationships and solidarity

Collective decision-making enhances all the values that have been discussed in preceding chapters. The idea of humanness in *ubuntu* captures all the qualities that can positively build organisations. All people like to know that they are important in an organisation. Collective decision-making strengthens relationships among colleagues and they pick up that each depends upon the other.

Employees can also see that the organisation depends upon them for survival. The solidarity displayed by the spiritual values of *ubuntu* illustrate that such values can lead to co-operation and survival of the organisation.

When in an African village, people declare that "I am because you are" it is a declaration that we are together – when I am making decisions it is for us. Collective decision-making and relationships gives people a sense of security. People tend to understand why they are sharing the same space. The strengthening of relationships also strengthens the hope of attaining the goals of the organisation together.

5.3 Sharing power

Ubuntu and collective decision-making give us a sense of sharing power. The sharing of power within the organisation means that all employees are equal. We know there will be various people who occupy various positions in an organisation: the CEO, line managers, general employees and so on. But when it comes to decision-making in an *ubuntu*-driven organisation, the organisation becomes flat. All the inputs are crucial.

In organisations today, many critics are talking about the need to create more leaders in the workplaces. Therefore, a manager and his management team build other employee leaders within the staff. This is crucial for the improvement of the entire organisation. This may also be a good strategy in preparing people for succession.

5.4 Mutual understanding

Collective understanding cannot be realised without mutual understanding. When people understand one another in the workplace, this can pay dividends for production of the organisation. Mutual understanding includes all the qualities discussed that are part of communalism. Mutual understanding implies a number of characteristics such as:

- Collaboration
- Communalism
- Consensus
- Communication

Collective decision-making cannot be achieved when there is no mutual understanding among the people. Mutual understanding helps people not to talk over the other. It is also people who have learnt to work together, who live in a communal way, who will be amenable to shared decision-making.

The most useful word in mutual understanding is consensus. The community tries to reach consensus even when there are one or two people who see things differently. The community tries to reach common ground. This is vital in a workplace. Employees need to reach consensus so as to be able to come to decisions.

Consensus implies solidarity. It also implies that even if people differ they negotiate the middle ground. Consensus eliminates hatred and hostility because it is based on how the majority sets the direction that the team needs to take.

5.5 Building better teams

Ubuntu is based on team culture, which ignites unity and peace in the workplace. It is not possible to be in a real team without being able to forge strong relationships.

Literature around organisational behaviour has emphasised the usefulness of teams in building organisations. *Ubuntu* is by nature about building a community of team members who drive towards the same goal. When people are together as a team, it is difficult to break their spirit. A strong team will not be easy to break because it carries the spirit of the community.

An old African folktale tells of an old man who gave his five warring sons a stick each to break. The sons were always fighting each other in the household. All of them found it easy to break the stick given to them by the old man. However, the old man now took five sticks and tried them together in a bundle. None of the sons was able to break the bundle of sticks. The old man explained, "When you are together as one, nothing will ever break you. Do not fight each other because you will be scattered, alone and vulnerable. Be one, be a team."

The old man's tale shows how important teams can be in society. There are reasons why organisations build teams:

- They want the employees to focus on a vision. A team works well when there is a vision that they are working towards. Strong organisations work towards a vision.

- They want organisations to share common goals. When teams play in a field of players, they all have one goal – to win. All the team players share the common goal although they play different positions in the team. It takes the solidarity of the team to reach its goal.

- They work within the leadership of the organisation. Effective leaders and managers are aware that it is through effective teams that they can enhance the work of the organisation. Leaders want work done and it is for the good of the organisation when this is done by all those involved.

- They create the "collective self" of the organisation. In *ubuntu*, organisations need the collective self to illustrate the community's plans.

- They symbolise the crucial nature of the group in running the organisation.

- Teams reinforce commitment. When teams have common goals and shape the vision mentioned above, they become more committed to organisational functionality. Teams can be useful in enhancing the culture of the organisation.

Effective teams are necessary for all organisations. There are various ways suggested on how to build effective teams that will uphold the norms of success. The University of California's *Guide to Managing Human Resources*[61] lists the following as crucial in building an effective team:

- Consider each employee's ideas as valuable: there is no stupid idea in the organisation.

- Be aware of the employee's unspoken feelings: there is a need to be open with employees and sensitive to their feelings.

- Act as a harmonising influence: mediation and resolution of conflicts is crucial in working teams.

- Be clear when communicating: clear directives should be given at all times.

- Encourage trust and co-operation among employees in your team: when there are strong relationships in the workplace, people will work together.

- Encourage team members to share information: employees need to understand that all their positions are a network whose collective goals lead to the accomplishment of the same vision.

- Delegate problem-solving task to the team: teams should find solutions together.

- Facilitate communication: successful teams need effective communication. Effective teams will use today's channels of communication such as email, Twitter, Facebook and WhatsApp among others.

- Establish team values and goals: talking to members and discussing what the team needs is crucial and may steer the organisation to success.

- Evaluate team performance: team members should always understand their roles at all times.

- Ensure that you have a clear idea of what you need to accomplish: members should not doubt what their mission and vision is. These must be communicated well.

- Use consensus: consensus may take a long time but it provides a platform where better decisions can be made.

- Set ground rules for the team: norms should be established for team members to understand their route to success.

- Establish a method for arriving at a consensus: professionally maturity means that employees will be able to arrive at a consensus. Managers should prepare their employees for this as part of employee development.

- Encourage listening and brainstorming: in chapter 3 we discussed the importance of listening in organisations. This needs to be encouraged so that employees do not talk across one another.

- Establish the parameters of consensus-building sessions.

Managers should be sensitive to the frustration that can build when the team is not achieving consensus. Furthermore, managers should also be careful of false consensus and try to find out the individuals' real feelings.

Effective teams will instil the above as the employees chase the vision of their organisation. Frequently, managers have to concede that certain values such as those highlighted above will strengthen the *ubuntu* principles.

5.6 Using humanness to chase a vision

For years, African communities have exercised *ubuntu* as a form of management. From time immemorial *ubuntu* shows collective decision-making. As highlighted under building teams, chasing a vision is crucial. Collective decision-making depends upon the use of ethics.

The use of humanness in chasing the vision entails the following:

- Shared concern
- Wisdom
- Justice
- Using human nature and warmth.

Effective leaders will embrace the *ubuntu* characteristics as they train their employees to be receptive to *ubuntu* styles of leadership.

> This chapter demonstrated the following:
>
> - That collective decision-making is crucial in *ubuntu*-driven organisations.
>
> - Organisations should be able to use diversity as it instils *ubuntu* values.
>
> - Collective decisions lead to effective teamwork.
>
> - Collective decisions are the basis of solidarity in organisations.
>
> - An organisational vision can be more easily attained through a collective decision-making processes.

CHAPTER SIX

PRODUCTION

6.1 Introduction

Table 6.1 The Five Ps of ubuntu – **Production**

Ubuntu – The Five Ps				
People-centredness	Permeable walls	Partisanship	Progeny	Production

Chapter 2 discussed the role of people-centredness in the workplace. It displays the value of elevating the roles of relationships and emphasising different roles in the workplace.

Some people may wrongly think that in such an environment work is sacrificed to magnify relationships. A leader may be thought to forget about the core business of the company as he focuses on compassion and friendliness. In this chapter we look at how the cultural values of *ubuntu* support the core business of an organisation.

When the village goes to the fields to sow seeds, it is with the spirit of *ubuntu*. All the villagers are committed and look forward to the reaping season. The villagers are committed because they know that if they do not stay focused on reaching the goal, and enhancing production, they will all go hungry. Supporting the production of the organisation is linked to all the other four Ps that have been discussed previously.

Employees produce because of:

- **People-centredness** – doing it for others. Not letting down the team, each person does his/her own share of work.

- **Permeable walls** – the roles are communicated all the time. People know what needs to be done because there is constant and effective communication.

- **Partisanship** – all became loyal to team goals. The people are loyal to the brand of the organisation.

- **Progeny** – the leader may initiate decisions but they patter down throughout the organisation through consultation. It is via this collective ownership of decisions that everyone shares similar goals for ensuring production.

The democratic nature portrayed by *ubuntu* cultural values ensures that people own the decisions to produce more for the company. People know real production means much for the entire village as well as themselves. The collective commitment embedded in the employees in an *ubuntu* environment ensures that they produce according to the organisation's vision. The collective commitment gives rise to the collective solidarity and awareness in every employee that if I do not put in an extra effort, I am failing the village, the company.

From the beginning of each year, when the organisation plans, each employee must have an individual year plan which should fit within the team's year plan. The interdependence in an *ubuntu*-driven organisation demonstrates that there is collective ownership when failure to produce at the end comes. Yet, when success comes, all reap from the rewards because each individual is part of the longer chain of the organisation.

Ubuntu values are the strength that leads to more production: solidarity, collective decision-making, compassion, sharing, building relationships and various other similar values that will be briefly discussed later in the chapter. The *ubuntu* values make it a point that the organisation achieves many of its set goals.

The actual and symbolic links among the people are most important virtues that lead to the production of the village. The virtuous aspect about *ubuntu* in the workplace is that people share the challenges and successes of the organisation too. Short time, less demand for the organisation's goods, and people who act differently from the expected cultural values are all factors that can debilitate the organisation. Yet true *ubuntu* cultural values will instil mature professional ways of responding to any ills through values such as collective responsibility, endurance, common understanding, holding one another's hand with the basic *ubuntu* tenet at the back of the head that, "I am because you are."

This chapter focuses on how companies use *ubuntu* by increasing gains and expanding the brand.

6.2 Ubuntu and performance at work

Thus far this book has shown the various parts of *ubuntu* cultural values in operation at work. But like all other workplaces, an *ubuntu*-driven workplace seeks to achieve excellence through production. Pio *et al*[62] show how productivity can be achieved differently under Western management and *ubuntu* indigenous management:

Productivity and efficiency in the traditional Western leadership/management perspectives are defined in terms of the ratio between production output and input cost. Maximising productivity is the raison d'être of organisation in the Western management tradition. Everything is about limiting costs and producing faster and promoting competition among employees, who are considered to be input costs.

Needless to say, this attitude contributes to fractured relationships, which contradicts the core belief under *ubuntu* that humans should take care of one another. In *ubuntu* the priority is on peaceful, harmonious coexistence and social well-being of fellow humans, productivity and efficiency become an outcome rather thant the raison d'etre of the organisation, and optimism of productivity and efficiency therefore becomes of operational goal. In times of economic downturns, for instance, employees would rather take across-the-board pay cuts than hold on to their current salaries at the expense of having their co-workers laid off as would be the recourse in Western management practice.

But all these need a strong leader who constantly demonstrates *ubuntu* values to all employees. It should be easy to see *ubuntu* spiritual values embraced by employees who internalise this for productivity as well. Sometimes productivity can be low in the workplace but we can sometimes fail to diagnose problems.

What causes the negative effects on production? A number of reasons can be the cause for low production;

- Uncertainty – when there is no clear communication and employees are not sure whether they have a job or not tomorrow.

- Culture and climate that are not conducive. A hostile environment will breed unwilling workers. (Later in this chapter we look at how leaders can manipulate culture to suit *ubuntu* cultural values).

- No motivation – unmotivated employees will not produce the set targets. Again later in this chapter we will focus on motivation.

In my study of organisational leadership and production over the past two decades I have discovered 11 ways that effective leaders use to motivate their employees and these are relevant to all workplaces:

i. Magnifying the goal of the village;

ii. Building strong communication channels;

iii. People need a strong leader;

iv. Employees need to be constantly supported;

v. Without set targets the village will not accomplish its goals;

vi. *Ubuntu* requires all to work within teams;

vii. People should have reason to come to work;

viii. An effective team is a team with the right tools;

ix. Constant professional development is necessary;

x. Productive employees are mentored;

xi. Magnifying the brand.

I briefly explain these below:

i. Magnifying the goal of the organisation – all employees need to be reminded all the time about the collective goal. This need not be verbal: the culture, the mission statement and the spirit can be constant reminders to employees.

ii. Build strong communication channels – it helps when employees know what to do at all times. Uncertainty can confuse employees.

iii. Even in the village people need a strong leader – people need a person who leads the way and tells people what needs to be done. But this does not undermine respect and acknowledgement of the dignity of the employees.

iv. Employees need to be supported – workers bring to work all sorts of problems from their homes and communities. Some may not share their problems. But it is a supportive workplace that sees employees as community members who need to be linked to all. Supported workers are motivated workers. It is these workers who will drive productivity.

v.   Without targets the company cannot win. A good organisation will always set realistic goals.

vi. *Ubuntu* requires all to work in teams – *ubuntu* is about relationships, about togetherness and about openness. *Ubuntu-*driven organisations work through strong teams where employees equip one another with skills.

vii. People should have a reason to come to work – happy employees will do the best job all the time. It is difficult when employees are unhappy at any workplace. This affects production heavily. Later in the chapter we look at what stress can do to productivity.

viii. An effective team is a team with all the relevant implements – in the digital age people need the right tools at work. Cell phones, computers and various digital gadgets will help employees to complete work on time. Without the necessary tools workplaces can delay production and create disgruntled employees.

ix. Constant professional development – again with the advent of the digital age, things change fast. It is necessary to constantly train or develop employees on new skills.

x.   Productive employees are mentored – it is one of the most crucial factors for successful workplaces. Effective mentors will help employees to cope with the constant changes in workplaces. Mentors can also ensure that when employees face challenges they will be able to withstand the challenges.

xi. Magnifying the brand – it is difficult to make the clients believe in the company's brand when the employees do not. The organisation should always ensure that the employees understand their brand and are proud of it. Effective leaders will know what to add in their organisations to make them come top.

A.T. Martins[63] also lists 12 ways to improve employees' productivity:

i. Make all employees accountable for their goals and their assignments – leaders need to specific when delegating duties.

ii. Ensure that you follow up with them about progress at various stages – leaders need to follow up on tasks delegated.

iii. Avoid micromanaging while managing people; remember they are humans, not machines – employees need the best working environment.

iv. Encourage reward, motivate and recognise all jobs well done – employees are motivated by a pat on the back for a job well done.

v. Reach out to all employees working for you – employees want to be treated well, leaders need to show compassion.

vi. Set realistic and achievable targets for the workers – leaders should always set attainable goals.

vii. Encourage team work for better results – leaders should break isolation because in teams employees can inspire one another.

viii. Make sure that people enjoy their work and are happy to come to work every day – the working environment should be a happy environment.

ix. Do not let a task become monotonous and boring – leaders should rotate people in different jobs according to their expertise.

x. Sponsor your employees for courses; send them to programmes that will help them improve their skills – employees' skills need to be improved to enhance productivity.

xi. Do not waste too much time behind closed doors; spending hours in meetings when that time could be spent on delivering results – effective time management is crucial.

xii. Make sure that you provide your employees with time saving and efficiency enhancing devices like laptops, smartphones and other digital devices – they can help employees to save time and be productive.

The *ubuntu*-driven workplace can follow these to enhance productivity. The culture in *ubuntu* promotes diligence and collective responsibility. People appreciate respect and dignity shown in the organisation. In any workplace job satisfaction is crucial. People will leave an organisation when they are not satisfied.

6.3 Strong organisational values

Employees in an *ubuntu*-driven workplace experience a number of factors that have been explored at length in this book. Of the many values we have mentioned are solidarity, collective management, honesty and relationships. Effective leaders will build and increase these positive values, which will lead to employee loyalty: strong organisations have their employees' loyalty. Employee loyalty is critical for production and leaders could use *ubuntu* to create an invitational and welcoming culture to lure their employees.

Good leaders:

- Promote a caring environment.
- Build an invitational atmosphere.
- Are interested in their employees.
- Open opportunities for growth.

These make the employees be loyal and be interested in their workplace, and result in workers who feel valued, who have access to the ladder of promotion and are working in effective teams.

This chapter has looked into a number of elements that promote productivity. All the various factors discussed in this book have a huge effect on productivity. Employees who love what they do and love the workplace environment will thrive. Their performance constantly improves as they enhance production. A good workplace environment creates intrinsic motivation among employees. Incentives and rewards work well but when these are removed sometimes they tend to leave uncommitted workers.

The factors below are part of *ubuntu* philosophy and encourage intrinsic motivation.

- Honesty
- Inspiration
- Collective decision-making
- Respect
- Dignity
- Openness.

When these factors are applied consistently in organisations, they bring the best out of employees. The company leaders should plan these. Running an organisation needs to be planned well. Appropriate roles given to employees will always improve their capability and make them happy.

Below the discussion is on five aspects that are important in enhancing production. These are improvement of workplace culture, demonstration of leadership, investing in training/ development, power of delegation and overcoming stress.

6.4 Improving work place culture and the role of the leader

We have read in several sections of the book already of how *ubuntu*'s inherent qualities have a potential to improve workplace culture. Managers need to lead the process of fostering this *ubuntu* culture in their organisations.

Effective cultures will motivate employee performance, commitment and dedication. Subsections 6.2 and 6.3 above spell out elements that can enhance workplace culture. Managers will use certain values in improving their companies or organisations. Organisations are part of society hence their value systems should be developed with this in mind.

For *ubuntu* culture there needs to be a methodical preparation of the employees. Below, is a cycle of improving organisational culture that managers can use to forge an *ubuntu* workplace culture:

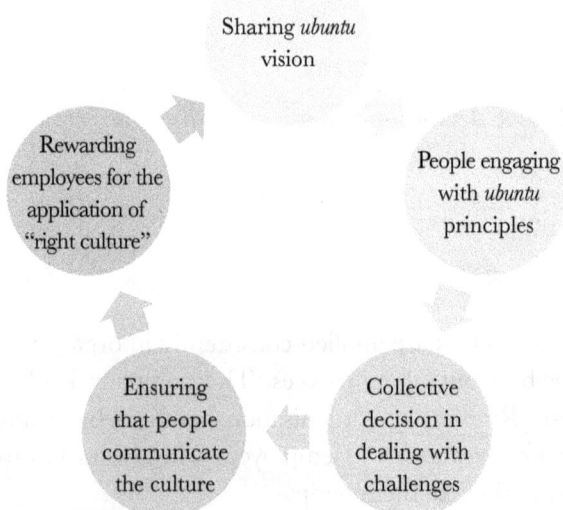

Figure 6.1 Ubuntu fostering cycle (for production)

The above cycle illustrates how managers can lead people-centred production in the workplace. The *ubuntu* model also displays how people-focused approaches can be merged with production for the organisation. Below, the cycle is briefly explained.

6.4.1 Sharing *ubuntu* vision

Employees need to understand what their vision is all the time. Managers should share the vision they have of the organisation to employees at all times. Even the best of visions will not work if the employees do not know what goals and targets they are supposed to look towards. The vision explains the existence of the organisation and it explains its strategic goals and action plans.

An *ubuntu*-based vision guides and inspire employees to work towards the core values of *ubuntu* discussed in this book. They do all these to achieve the set goals. The *ubuntu*-inspired vision spells out the long-term goals of the organisation and inspires employees to embrace certain qualities as they embrace the organisation's vision.

Managers need to share the vision as it helps to attract employees and retain them. It helps employees to have a picture of a destination where they want to end up. When managers share the vision, they share a desired future of the organisation that is not dependent upon the managers only, but the entire team.

6.4.2 People engaging with *ubuntu* principles

Any vision will be as good as its implementation. Effective managers wanting to increase production will engage their staff in strengthening the envisaged *ubuntu* principles. When people engage with the principles of *ubuntu*, they will learn to share a sense of purpose and embrace a shared understanding of what the organisation stands for.

When people engage with the principles they also learn to reinvent themselves as they understand the bigger picture and create a positive culture. When managers engage employees, they also help in the development of various other qualities such as passion and enthusiasm. Engaging employees also means that they would be able to appreciate the spirit of *ubuntu* and its application in the workplace and collectively focus on what they should be achieving.

6.4.3 Collective decision-making in dealing with challenges

Again, collective decision-making has been emphasised in various chapters in this book and we know that in an organisation where there is no collective decision among employees it is difficult to think of productivity. This collective decision in looking at productivity ensures that teams will bring positive culture in an organisation.

The building of a team culture in any organisation may lead to the accomplishment of set goals. Collective decision-making also ensures that employees look at various alternatives as they discuss the shaping of their organisation.

Challenges will always appear in organisations and it helps when a group rather than an individual decides on a way forward. It is true, though, that sometimes decisions have to be made quickly rather than follow a tedious process of calling the group. However, even when management has to make decisions these need to be explored by the general group of employees. Challenges in organisations affect all and this is the reason all employees have to be considered in deciding. Collective decision-making engenders a culture of trust and transparency in an organisation.

6.4.4 Ensure that people communicate the culture

The training and preparation of employees for the *ubuntu* organisation has been another huge emphasis in this book. Managers manipulate the culture of an organisation in several ways and among these is the training of employees. *Ubuntu* models expect people to be flexible to change: an organisation that deals with people should be able to accommodate them.

People who are flexible can embrace failure and learn to move the organisation forward. In a culture of communication as explored in depth in chapter 3, people are able to understand one another well. Effective communication creates a culture of collaboration. Successful teams use effective communication to come up with winning formulae. When a culture has good communication, it ensures that all employees become aware of their targets and that is crucial for attaining the vision.

6.4.5 Rewarding employees for application of the "right culture"

When organisations want to encourage their employees they introduce systems where employees are appreciated and rewarded. This may be good in motivating a winning team that constantly follows a vision and a working culture. Management needs to reward employees and all employees need to benefit in an *ubuntu*-inspired workplace if they follow the basic principles and the vision of the organisation. Rewarding employees is not only about giving them cash. Excelling employees can be mentioned in staff meetings, or an email could be circulated company-wide, recognising an employee.

> **Think of other ways in which employees can be recognised for their contribution in an organisation.**

Working with the organisation's culture is the first step towards the realisation of a working organisation. Authors in South Africa have referred to underperforming organisations as institutions that have anomalies in culture; a breakdown in the culture of working and production. Without a culture that feeds into the work ethic of the organisation, nothing will be achieved by organisations. The organisational culture influences staff behaviour and how they see their role in fulfilling the organisation's vision. A number of positive concepts tossed around in organisation literature include shared leadership, collaboration and collegiality. But these cannot be realised in organisations where a conducive culture is not evident. Successful organisations have certain distinguishing qualities.

6.5 Time management

Today's organisations need the careful management of time. Time is a crucial element and it sustains successful organisations. Managers should respect time and ensure that the employees also manage time well. Time management is one of the most important skills that employees need to keep because it has a great impact on organisational goals but it needs:

- Commitment of self and team
- Setting routine
- Being able to prioritise
- Planning ahead.

Managers can use daily, weekly or monthly planners to ensure that time is used well in the workplace. David Bakke[64] mentions five aspects that need to be considered when planning effective time management:

i. Eliminate the unnecessary: anything that is an obstacle, which makes others not reach certain goals, should be shoved aside.

ii. Plan your work: set time aside before work to plan by writing down or plan mentally what you want to achieve. After planning, one can start executing the duties to be performed.

iii. Multitasking: this is a skill some people have. When employees can, they should try and multitask. But when they can't, they should not force it, because it can cause more delays.

iv. Know when to multitask: those who can multitask should know when to use this skill.

v. Reduce interruptions: employees need to minimise the number of disturbances that can steal their focus. Finding a quieter place to work or any other way to block distractions can help in time management.

The various values that are discussed in this book enhance time management and are effective for production:

- Strong teams
- Shared vision
- Shared Leadership
- Solidarity
- Meaningful collegial ties
- Commitment
- Goal directedness.

> **Which other qualities can you think of?**

In an *ubuntu*-driven organisation collective decision-making should help employees discuss the best ways of managing time well for the organisation. The organisation should generate new rituals to engender the spirit of *ubuntu*. Lazy employees will never have a sense of time. Employees who are not respected are unlikely to respect time. Time management needs a holistic view of the organisation. Managers need to plan a culture that supports good time management. When some members do not care about time management in an organisation, they are killing the common good of *ubuntu*.

6.6 Investing in development/training

Successful organisations train their workers all the time because of continuous developments that occur in the world. All organisations, whether using the *ubuntu* model or not, need production, and to enhance relationships and build a community of content employees. Training is necessary for the following reasons:

- Building upon employee strengths. There are many talented and diligent employees who need the support of management to enhance these. Effective managers will identify employees with strengths and use this to the benefit of the organisation and that of the employee.

- Shared leadership and shared vision need proper preparation. Again, effective managers will prepare their employees for an organisation based on principles of sharing the vision as well as leadership. *Ubuntu*-driven organisations need this all the time.

- Trust increases production. In organisations where there is mistrust, workers are not motivated to work hard. They can do the minimum they have to do but not go further than that. Organisations need to train staff in the importance of transparency, honesty and ethical living. When employees are trusted by fellow employees in turn they trust them. This builds relationships and increase production.

- Training the trainer and sharing skills. Companies can cut much expenditure by using their own employees to train others. Organisations need to have a programme of sharing skills. New employees should not struggle and should always get the support of experienced employees. This is also linked to mentoring. Effective workplaces would prepare other gifted workers to welcome and assist others.

Training should not be haphazard but needs to be planned well. Investing in training is planning for the success of the organisation. When done well, this will have a long-term positive impact upon the entire organisation. During the planning process and actual training, communication needs to be ongoing.

One major factor we need for successful training is the SOAR analysis which may be used to replace the overused SWOT analysis. Many new organisations tend to prefer the use of SOAR than SWOT because of the forward-looking nature of this analysis. It enables managers and the employees to look at the organisation differently.

6.7 SOAR the winning organisation

The acronym SOAR refers to **S**trengths, **O**pportunities, **A**spirations and **R**esults. An organisation that uses SOAR analysis focuses on its current strengths as a well as its vision.

SOAR analysis is different from SWOT analysis because among others SWOT tends to reinforce the top-down approach. SOAR can be used by all the people in the organisation to enhance the strengths of the team and the vision of the collective. SOAR analysis seeks to address aspects that are pertinent to any organisation's growth.

Each of the letters represents the following:

S	addresses the strengths of the organisation. These are aspects or factors that make the organisation tick.
O	addresses the opportunities, the positive aspects the organisation uses as it strives in moving forward.
A	addresses the destination the organisation wants to move towards. An organisation can choose from a number of paths. Members should be able to aspire and choose certain preferred paths. These are the paths that would ensure that the vision is attained.
R	addresses the accomplishment of the organisation. Has it attained the measurable results set out at the beginning?

SOAR analysis is crucial for production and should be applied to the organisation at all times. Many people are critical of the SOAR model, however, because they claim that it appears to overlook the threats and weaknesses as the focus is more on the positive factors.

> **What do you think of the need to focus on the organisation's weaknesses when you analyse your organisation? What are your views on SOAR analysis as compared to SWOT analysis?**

This may be said to be akin to *appreciative leadership* where leaders want to build on the organisation's good qualities. SOAR is based on principles that illustrate that the organisation can emphasise the following:

- Leaders can use the organisation's strengths.
- They can ensure that the employees continuously add to the positives that already exist in the organisation
- Appreciating the aspirations and future of the organisation.
- Driving towards measurable results.

Ubuntu leadership has a number of common qualities with appreciative leadership. In their ground-breaking book Diana Whitney, Amanda Trosten-Bloom and Kae Rader[65] list five strategies of Appreciative Leadership that people need to embrace:

- To know they belong
- To feel valued for what they have to contribute
- To know where the organisation or community is headed
- To know that excellence is expected and can be depended on
- To know that they are contributing to the general good.

The above are based on:

> *The wisdom of inquiry* – people should know that they are valued.

> *The art of illumination* – people should understand how they can contribute to the organisation.

The genius of inclusion – people are made to understand how they can contribute to the organisation.

The courage of inspiration – people move toward a sense of direction because there are goals.

The path of integrity – people give their best for success.

These may be used in SOAR analysis to promote positive power within the organisation. It may increase production through the stimulation of employee confidence. The focus needs to be on what drives the organisation towards success.

Prepare a diverse training team

Training does not need to be formal all the time. Continuous training can happen informally throughout the organisation all year round. Colleagues can also train their colleagues in informal settings. It is important, however, that the training team needs to be diverse, because there are so many skills demanded by today's workplaces.

Share goals with employees

Before training can happen, workers need to know and even be able to criticise the programme if they so wish. It needs to address exactly what they feel needs to be done. Any programme of training will falter when employees do not endorse it. When this has been done, training can begin. It is important that during training, the employees can note any points of concern that require their attention.

Feedback from employees and trainers

Management needs to get proper feedback from both trainers and employees. Training can be the backbone of an organisation. When done correctly, it can advance the goals of the organisation. More importantly, it can lead to satisfied employees.

Communicate way forward

After information has been generated, management needs to chart the way forward. Communication has been stressed in chapters 3 and 4. This can be used well when communicating where the organisation should go. It helps to give employees incentives after completion of formal training programmes. This should be communicated and discussed with employees long before the beginning of a programme.

6.8 Power of delegation

Managers need to delegate from time to time but they should do this when necessary and delegate to the right people in an organisation. It may kill an employee's spirit when they are delegated to functions they cannot perform. The trap that many managers who are meticulous fall into is not to delegate because they think that delegated duties won't be done to their satisfaction.

I once conducted a study on organisational leadership in KwaZulu-Natal. The manager was a workaholic whose company worked so hard with diligent teams. The head office was saying that this was among the top branches in the KwaZulu-Natal district. However, the employees were complaining that the manager was not delegating enough. No wonder it was difficult to find him sitting down in his office, because he was not delegating as he should: he was overworking himself. His problem was that he did not believe that his colleagues would do a perfect job when he delegated the job for them to do.

When proper training of employees has been done, there is no way that a manager cannot trust his employees. Delegation makes sense when employees are empowered to do the work. With the necessary skills, employees will be content in doing delegated duties. Mind Tools[66] [online] asks five questions that determine whether or not a manager needs to delegate:

i) Is there someone else who has (or can be given) the necessary information or expertise to complete the task? Essentially, is this a task that someone else can do or is it critical that you do it yourself?

ii) Does the task provide an opportunity to grow and develop another person's skills?

iii) Is this a task that will recur in a similar form in the future?

iv) Do you have enough time to delegate the job effectively? Time must be available for adequate training, for questions and answers, for opportunities to check progress, and for rework if that is necessary.

v) Is this a task that I should delegate? Tasks critical for long term success (for example, recruiting the right people for your team) genuinely do need your attention.

If a manager responded 'yes' to any of those, it means that the job may need delegation. In an open, transparent organisation, where employees are professionally matured, management will give them responsibilities without fear of underperformance or non-delivery. There is no need for managers to overburden themselves with work when they should delegate.

Employees become discontent when there is no delegation. Non-delegation of duties shows that they are not trusted. Managers who do not delegate risk having employees who will not give their support in the organisation.

Ubuntu-driven organisations will have the qualities of trust, honesty and solidarity discussed before, to spur delegation of duties. Yet the other extreme is over-delegation, which should not be done because it can be detrimental to the team. With this, the organisation may fail, as members may not be able to use their abilities because they are overstretched or given work that is beyond their capability. Delegation needs to be appropriate for the employees and when it is not it can be dangerous for the organisation's survival.

Before delegating duties, managers should ask themselves the right questions:

- Does the employee understand the delegated duty?
- Am I not setting him/her up for failure?
- Have I communicated what needs to be done well?
- Will there be enough support should the employee need it?

When decisions are made collectively in an organisation, these are easily addressed. Like any other, delegation needs to be planned in conjunction with the employees. It needs to be part of organisational development.

6.9 Emotional intelligence

Generally, *ubuntu* can adapt to this "Western" concept of emotional intelligence. It is critical for managers to use emotional intelligence to lead a working organisation that would accomplish set goals.

Using emotional intelligence in an *ubuntu*-driven organisation, managers and employees will be mindful of pertinent *ubuntu* aspects such as managing relationships, working in teams, sharing vision and everything linked to this culture. Effective managers will create a relevant culture in the workplace when they respect the employees.

Employees tend to like their workplace when they see that their managers accommodate them even when they differ from them. In fact, good managers embrace all employees, including those they differ with. All these form the basis of crucial emotional intelligence. Managers and their employees who focus on emotional intelligence actually look at relationship dynamics in an organisation, and try to motivate others as they improve their skills.

Emotional intelligence ensures that managers who portray positive aspects of their emotions can make others have these as well. All employees should be able to gauge other people's emotions. Even in teams, emotional intelligence equips us to be able not only to identify and control our emotions but also respond to other fellow employees' emotions. This means that there is much need for employees to understand themselves well if emotional intelligence can be applied well to enhance productivity.

Positive attitudes and strong relationships are cornerstones of healthy emotional intelligence. Blaming and being aggressive to others will not feature among those who are emotionally intelligent. Managers who accommodate emotional intelligence will work closely with the qualities embedded in *ubuntu*. *Ubuntu* is about being understood by others and understanding them in return.

6.10 Maturity summit

From the first chapter this book has been emphasising the need for employees to be matured if they are to be able to be receptive to the *ubuntu*-driven organisation. This is the essence of this book and this was explained well in the first chapter where the adapted model from John Maxwell[67] showed the importance of matured employees in a workplace. As I close this chapter I focus on what I refer to as the *Maturity Summit*, which shows two aspects in maturity: the ascending and the descending sides overleaf. To reach the pinnacle of maturity the new employee ascends the mountain as they learn about the dynamics of the organisation. Then after reaching the summit they need to descend the mountain. Descending the mountain is a time of reflection, of ensuring that one understands the organisation well.

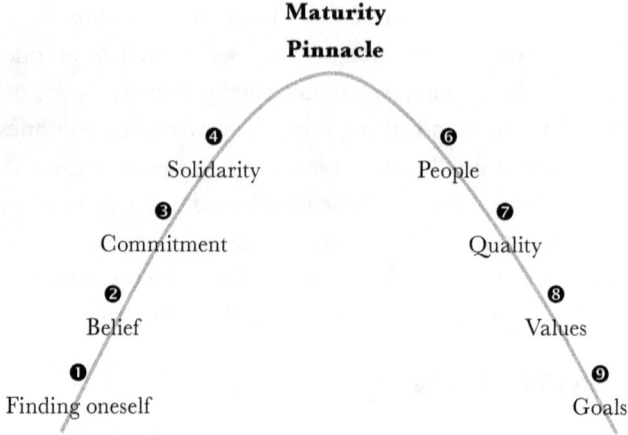

Fig 6.2 Maturity Summit

6.10.1 Finding oneself

This is the first step of the ascending side and is part of the development process. They are new at a company and they are trying to find themselves as they try to learn more about themselves and their colleagues. They still want to understand why they are in this workplace.

6.10.2 Belief

As people are shown the mission and vision of the organisation they learn beliefs, cultures and climate of their workplace. They also learn cultures and some of these they have to overlook.

6.10.3 Commitment

Almost every chapter here has emphasised the need for commitment. New employees should learn the culture of commitment.

6.10.4 Solidarity

In *ubuntu*-driven organisations employees will have learnt nothing if they cannot understand the value of solidarity and collectiveness in the workplace. Understanding the need for solidarity means they understand the essence of *ubuntu*.

6.10.5 Maturity

This is the summit and when a new employee reaches the summit they are matured and they understand what *ubuntu*-driven organisations are all about. They understand how to be an employee who is able to work in teams and able to engage in collective decision-making. These employees are people-centred, are loyal and can serve their organisations with pride.

6.10.6 People

In chapter 2 we discussed the importance of people-centredness. In this first stage of descending, understanding people is crucial in a time of reflection. The employee should take time to think about how they relate to fellow employees. In *ubuntu* you exist because there are other people. The organisation will be sustained by this mutual understanding which also has deep implications for production.

6.10.7 Quality

Any organisation that serves customers has to ensure that quality is supreme. It may not be important to produce more quantity when the quality is wanting. Quality reflects what the community wants in the organisation. High performing teams will produce good quality. When a client sees the quality of the product, s/he sees the employees in the product. Happy employees will worry about quality in the organisation. Again, good managers will make their employees satisfied in a free environment where they are recognised as people.

6.10.8 Values

The managers and their employees should constantly examine the relevance of their values. After a certain period values may need to be changed as the organisation grows in existence. Good values sustain organisations that produce good work. There are so many values necessary for excelling workplaces and many of these are part of *ubuntu* and have been discussed in previous chapters.

Solidarity, relationships, honesty, collaboration and transparency are among the critical values that should be major when reflecting about an organisation's production. When people think of reflect on the organisation they need to constantly think of which values to add to the community within the organisation.

Among the important values critical for production are those contained in the REAP values model:

R	**Respect**. Employees like to be respected as people. They will work hard when they know they are valued by management.
E	**Ethical living**. When employees do not care about the values of the organisation they may destroy the organisation. Yet, ethical living ensures that employees are serious about their morals at the workplace. An ethical employee will not steal or break working tools wilfully. Ethical workers know the implications of their morals in the company.
A	**Accountability.** Respected workers who lead ethical lives are also accountable in the organisation. When things do not go right, they take the blame and see what needs to be done to correct the wrong. Accountable employees work hard to produce their best in the workplace.
P	**Positive attitude**. Employees with a positive attitude will always focus on the goal as they support each other. Positive attitude is a value that helps the organisation even when it is sinking in difficult times.

6.10.9 Goals

The ultimate objective of production is accomplishing set goals. Managers should set attainable goals with the team. There are daily, weekly, monthly and yearly goals. It is always important to set goals that are within the range of the employees. It will not help if managers and their employees set unrealistic goals. During reflection time, the team needs to look at where they failed in setting realistic goals. Production will be negatively affected when the goals set are not attainable.

This penultimate chapter demonstrated the following:

- That high performance requires employees who are committed.
- The goals set by the organisation should be reachable.
- There are various ways to bolster productivity.
- Culture and values should be strengthened.
- Without time management the organisation will falter.
- The Maturity Summit needs to be realised as employees develop and later find time to reflect.

CHAPTER SEVEN

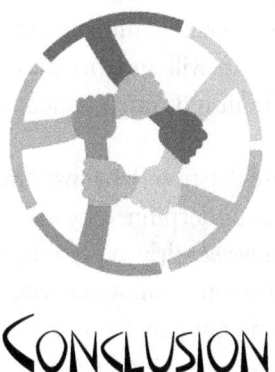

CONCLUSION

7.1 Closing comments

All organisations want to create workplaces that are not only productive but also boast employees who are satisfied with their jobs. The *ubuntu* paradigm is crucial in ensuring that the people in the organisation, the employees, are respected, as the working conditions are constantly improved.

I have used a village motif for the organisation or company throughout the book so that it can bring out the sense of the African setting. What is amazing with *ubuntu* is the oneness that characterises the organisation and the wonderful way in which the interconnectedness, solidarity, openness and various other qualities elucidated in this book have potential to lead to job satisfaction, thus ensuring that employees attain the organisation's goals.

The chapters in the book demonstrate how co-operation of the African spirit can enhance workplaces. The five Ps explored display how the community culture of *ubuntu* enhances relationships and team ethics that increase work commitment. As explained in previous chapters, the five Ps represent pertinent aspects of *ubuntu* way of life.

People-centredness, transparency, loyalty, collective decision-making and production are pivotal in all workplaces. Yet the major emphasis in the book is for teams to be committed and responsible if they are to attain these qualities.

Good teams also follow a set vision shared by all members of the organisation. However, as highlighted in chapter 1 it is effective, visionary managers who will support and nurture employees so that they become a matured, interconnected web that constantly strives for success.

This book has also illustrated that working organisations will be built on various values underpinned by *ubuntu*. Each conscientious, matured employee in *ubuntu*-driven organisations knows that when they fail, the organisation cannot succeed. In the village when some of the villagers do not play their role in ploughing during the season, the reaping season will be negatively affected.

The book also demonstrates the work that managers need to do in developing skills in the workplace and how empowered employees will create productive workplaces. Frequently, employees arrive at workplaces not having the necessary skills for the job. This may be compounded when they need to learn a new way of life such as *ubuntu*. Yet training is for all, including management, for in today's organisations all members need to be lifelong learners.

Ubuntu uses the human spirit that gives organisations the human face; people may have to be trained to understand this human face of the organisation. Reading through various models shows that there are *ubuntu* values that can be found in other Western models. The following contain elements found in *ubuntu*:

- Shared leadership
- Servant leadership
- Participatory leadership.

Yet the African humanism usually said to be synonymous with *ubuntu* gives it the qualities of a way of life that operates in a village or community. Throughout this book I have tried to reflect the workplace as that village or community where one would find compassion, collaboration and commitment. The chapters have also shown that in an *ubuntu* workplace we find:

- Closeness, but productivity
- Community, but individual support
- Loyalty, but the expression of voice
- Openness, but excellence
- Respect, but delivery
- Compassion, but commitment.

All these link up with the five Ps of *ubuntu* espoused in this book. But one cannot say that *ubuntu* management is the only way to working organisations. One can also not argue that productive organisations will be only those that use *ubuntu*-driven strategies. What this book professes is that in addition to other effective models, organisations may try to use what I refer to as the "African village model" of *ubuntu* because there is much to be learnt from the West and *ubuntu* models have much strength for sustaining better performing organisations.

Not only does *ubuntu* represent respect, community and openness, but it also represents communal justice. People in an *ubuntu* workplace know that they are protected in that community and that embracing *ubuntu* in the workplace is about transforming old, exclusively authoritarian systems. Organisations utilising *ubuntu* for example, may be able to transform the old top-down structure that characterised many organisations in the past.

Mbigi[68] declares that if a competitive, developed nation is to be built, collective solidarity in African life should find its expression in the modern forms of business entrepreneurship, business organisations and management. This author states that *ubuntu* is one philosophy that can help in developing practices of doing things together and differently in today's organisations. He also argues that South African organisations are faced with ruthless global competition hence the need to negotiate a shared common agenda in organisations. The book has also demonstrated how we need to build leadership around *ubuntu* values. Leaders and managers who adopt *ubuntu* approaches listen to employees and are understanding to various situations in the workplace. They are also able to create a working community.

7.2 Building a community

One of the main arguments in the previous chapters is the need to create a community with good human relations in the workplace. As stated several times in this text, communalism is pivotal in *ubuntu*-inspired workplaces. Furthermore, as illustrated in previous chapters, Khoza[69] points out that communalism is any of the several types of social organisation in which the individual is seen as being subordinate to a social collectivity such as state, a nation, a race or a social class. This author also argues that the concepts *ubuntu* and communalism have a potential of enhancing team participation as well as sharing of skills.

Mbigi[6] refers to a common vision within the *ubuntu* context as collective visioning. He also states that it is crucial in creating new collective mind set. The theory of shared leadership is one of the frequently discussed theories in literature; a theory that may demonstrate elements of collective development. Mbigi and Maree[70] refer to *ubuntu* as a spirit of collective development and reconstruction in organisations. Besides sharing a common vision within *ubuntu* context leads to the striking of a right balance between the individual and the group. The right balance between individualism and collectivism is made possible by accommodating people's need for dignity, self-respect and regard for others seriously.[71]

Nel *et. al.*[72] claims that shared vision is the deepest binding principle that enables employees to be united within an organisation. Common vision in the workplace ensures that employees are able to fight their doubts and fears. This is also important to achieve the organisation's goals and these qualities will lead employees to attain the necessary professional maturity.

7.3 Professional maturity and *ubuntu*

In chapter 1 the discussion shed light on why *ubuntu* needs professional maturity. Effective leaders need to prepare their employees for new changes within their organisations. *Ubuntu* will not thrive when people are not prepared for its adoption in the workplace.

The proliferation of Western models has made people shun other models because institutions have been generally run using Western models. The challenge of the leader, then, is to lead change initiatives in organisations.

Professionally matured employees display a number of qualities relevant to *ubuntu* spirit and wisdom. Professionally matured employees who can understand the five Ps of *ubuntu* show the following characteristics:

- They are success and vision driven
- They are accommodating and thoughtful of others
- They are able to think and work in teams although they can be independent and self-driven
- They value the rule of community
- They are not afraid of criticism but value being shown the right direction.

Organisations today need professionally matured employees to drive the success of their organisation. They have internalised the vision and aspirations of the managers and/or fellow employees. The managers need to constantly improve the skills of employees to enable them to gain professional maturity.

In chapter 6 I discussed emotional intelligence as one aspect that should be developed to enhance professional maturity; with this employees can support themselves as well as fellow workers. The professionally matured employee has a duty to support the immature colleagues who display these qualities:

- Lack of self-awareness
- Inability to follow a vision
- Inability to work with others
- Inability to see the collective aspirations of others.

Effective leaders will strive to create matured employees and the obvious is that they first need to be matured themselves. Managers who lack commitment and people skills cannot be professionally matured. This book shows how matured managers can use the five Ps of *ubuntu* to bring change in their organisations. Effective managers cultivate this maturity throughout the organisation amongst all employees.

7.4 Learning and sustenance of *ubuntu*

Among other challenges of leadership is the task of leading change. This is a time when leaders need to allay the fears of their employees. Facilitators of African leadership modules at universities might encounter a myriad of challenges. They need to prepare their students to welcome new learning and change. Many candidates in African-centred classrooms might be surprised, if not shocked, by knowledge that reflects the noble nature of African-centred knowledge.

It is not an easy process to change from an education system that shows the absolute dominance of Western model of education. Furthermore, Coghlan posits, "If change involves having to unlearn something in order to learn something new, and if the change involves giving up something to which the person has been previously committed or has valued, then it is expected that the process of change will be difficult."[73] Institutions of higher learning embracing indigenous knowledge systems and Africanisation need to think of a bigger role of re-educating Africans whose colonial history has convinced them to glorify Western traditions only.

Arguably, very few African students will believe in African leadership if they cannot be taught rigorously to appreciate themselves and the continent. Real transformation in Africa needs the reversal of many stereotypes and higher education should be at the forefront of transforming knowledge.[74] Furthermore, Vilakazi[75] points out that African intellectuals must initiate the formulation of a new and proper education policy for Africa. They need to engage in a process of re-education of themselves on the principles and patterns of African civilisation. Pityana[76] supports this as he states:

> The panorama of the South African higher education system can never be complete without resorting to what Van Ginkel refers to as the 'Copernican Revolution' – demanding a paradigm shift as revolutionary as the shift away from the Ptolemaic belief that the earth was at the centre of the universe. We dare to assert that there cannot be one centre of the knowledge universe but many, and that Africa has as much a claim to that centre as any other.

Teffo[77] points out that all that companies need is a mentor to teach or preach *ubuntu*. Teffo[78] also states that this will go a long way into answering the question of: "How do we incorporate *ubuntu* in our management style?" The idea of introducing a mentor is crucial, especially when one looks at the crucial aspect of preparing the workers as the climate is made conducive to be receptive to *ubuntu* models. *Ubuntu* empowers people to love and respect each other. In the search for a new management style, the writing of memos may have to be supplemented by communication (follow-up oral presentation and/or discussions). It would yield better results if the director or manager were to go to the people and discuss issues with them.

As we enter in the 21st century many leadership models have become crucial and among these are African models that incorporate philosophies such as *ubuntu*. The *ubuntu* worldview can have a positive impact when its principles are used effectively in leading any organisation. Yet *ubuntu* demands a paradigm shift, a change in what many employees have been used to. As literature illustrates above, much research has shown the potential of participative-based strategies. However, aspects such as caring, sharing, respect and compassion might be challenging to internalise for many workers. *Ubuntu* poses this challenge of fostering a culture of interconnectedness and interdependence among workers.

References

Bakke, D. *5 Effective time management tips. Techniques and skills you need to master*. [Online]. Available: http://www.moneycrashjers.com. [Accessed 13 March 2015].

Bottery, M. 2004. *The challenges of educational leadership*. London: Paul Chapman.

Coghlan D 1992. Renewal, re-education, and change. *The Furrow*, 43(4): 226-234.

Crafford, A. 2001. Communication. In S.P. Robbins., A. Odendaal., and G. Roodt (Eds.), *Organisational Behaviour: Global and Southern African Perspectives*. Cape Town: Pearson, pp. 223-240.

Dandala H.M. 1996. Cows never die: embracing African cosmology in the process of economic growth. . In: R Lessem, B Nassbaum (Eds.): *Sawubona Africa: Embracing Four Worlds in South African Management*. Sandton: Zebra, pp. 69-85.

Department of Education (DoE). 2001. *Manifesto on values, education and democracy*. Pretoria: Government Printer.

Dowding, K., Mergoupis, T., & Van Vugt, M. 2000. Exit, voice and loyalty: Analytic and Empirical developments. *European Journal of Political Research*, 37: 469-495.

Enslin, P., & Horsthemke, K. 2004. Can *ubuntu* provide a model for citizenship education in African democracies? *Comparative Education*, 40 (4), 545-557.

Farrell, D & Rusbult, C.E. 1992. Exploring the Exit, Voice, Loyalty and Neglect Typology: The influence of job satisfaction, quality of alternatives and investment size. *Employee Responsibilities and Rights Journal*, 5(3): pp.201-218.

Fusion, J. *How to change the culture of the workplace.* [Online]. Available:. http://smallbusiness.chron.com/change-culture-workplace. [Accessed 20 March 2015].

Goman, C.K. 2004. "This isn't the company I joined": How to lead in a business turned upside down. National City, CA: KCS Publishers.

Greenleaf, R.K. 2002. *Servant leadership: A journey into the nature of legitimate power and greatness.* New York: Paulist Press.

Hirschman, A.O. 1970. *Exit, Voice, and Loyalty: Responses to Decline in Firms, Organisations, and States.* Cambridge, MA: Harvard University Press.

Jazzar, M., & Algozzine, B. 2007. *Keys to Successful 21st Century Educational Leadership.* Boston: Pearson.

Khoza, R. 1994. The need for an Afrocentric approach to management. In Christie, P., Lessem, R. and Mbigi, L. (Eds). *African management: philosophies, concepts and applications.* Randburg: Knowledge Resources: p.117–124.

Kirshenbaum, H. 1995. *100 ways to enhance values and morality in schools and youth settings.* Boston: Allyn and Bacon.

Makgoba M.W. 1996. *Mokoko: The Makgoba affair: A reflection on transformation.* Florida: Vivlia.

Makhanya, M.S. 2011. *Ethical servant leadership at UNISA.* Keynote address at the Principal's summit Royal Elephant Hotel, July, 4, 2011.

Martins, A.T. *12 simple ways to improve employees' productivity.* [Online]. Available:http://www.mytopbusinessideas.com. [Accessed 17 March 2015].

Masango, M. 2002. Leadership in African context. *Verbum et ecclesia,* 23 (3):707-718.

Maxwell, J.C. 1993. *Developing the leader within you.* New York: Thomas Nelson.

Mbigi, L. & Maree, J. 2005. *Ubuntu: the spirit of African transformation management*. Randburg: Knowledge Resources.

Mbigi, L. 1997. *Ubuntu: the African dream in management*. Randburg: Knowledge Resources.

Mbigi, L. 2005. *In search of the African business renaissance: an African cultural perspective*. Randburg: Knowledge Resources.

Metz, T. 2011. *Ubuntu* as a moral theory and human rights in South Africa. *Africa Human rights law journal*, 11:532-559.

Miller, K. 2001. Values, Attitudes, and Job Satisfaction. In In S.P. Robbins., A. Odendaal., & G. Roodt (Eds.), *Organisational Behaviour: Global and Southern African Perspectives*. Cape Town: Pearson, pp 65-84.

MindTools. *Successful delegation*. [Online]. Available: www.mindtools,com. [Accessed 28 March 2015].

Mkandawire, T. 2005. Introduction. In T. Mkandawire, (Ed.), *African Intellectuals: Rethinking politics, Language, Gender and Development* (pp.1-9). London: Zed Books.

Msila, V. 2002. *Teachers as managers of Change*. Unpublished Doctoral Dissertation. Port Elizabeth: Vista University.

Mthembu, D. 1996. African values: Discovering the indigenous roots of management. In R. Lessem., & B. Nassbaum (Eds.), *Sawubona Africa: Embracing Four Worlds in South African Management*. Sandton: Zebra, pp. 215-226

Nel, C. 1994. Value-centred leadership – the journey to becoming a world-class. In P. Christie., R. Lessem., & L. Mbigi (Eds.), *African management: philosophies, concepts and applications*. Randburg: Knowledge Resources.

Ntuli, P. 1999. The missing link between culture and education: Are we still chasing Gods that are not our own? In M.W. Makgoba (Ed.), *African Renaissance*. Cape Town: Mafube, pp.184-199.

Peters T.J., & Waterman, R.H. 1982. *In search of excellence: Lessons from America's best-run companies*. Cambridge: Harper & Collins Publishers.

Pio, E., Waddock, S., Mangaliso, M., McIntosh, M., Spiller, C., Takeda, H., Gladstone, J., Ho, M., & Syed, O. 2012. Pipeline to the future: Seeking wisdom in indigenous, Eastern and Western Traditions. In J. Neal (Ed.), *Handbook of faith and spirituality in the workplace: Emerging research and practice*. New York: Springer, pp. 195-222.

Pityana, N.B. 2007. *Higher education, Transformation and Africanisation- A Paradigm Shift?* [Online]. Available: www.ieasa.studysa.org. [Accessed 10 August 2014].

Prinsloo, E.D. 1998. Ubuntu culture and participatory management. In Coetzee, P.H. and Roux, A.P.J. (Eds).*The African philosophy reader*. London: Routledge, pp.41–51.

Scott, W.G. & T.R. Mitchell. 1976. *Organisation Theory: A Structural and Behaviour Analysis.* Homewood, IL: Richard D. Irwin.

Sergiovanni, T.J. 2000. *The life world of leadership: creating culture, community, and personal meaning in our schools*. San Francisco: Jossey-Bass.

Teffo, L. 1999. Moral Renewal and African Experience(s). In M.W. Makgoba (Ed.), *African Renaissance*. Mafube: Cape Town.

The Wallace Foundation 2007. *A Wallace Perspective: Getting Principal Mentoring Right: Lessons from the Field*. New York: The Author

University of California San Francisco *Guide to managing human resources*. [Online]. Available:http:UCSfhn.UCSF.edu. [Accessed 2 May 2015].

Vilakazi, H. W. 2002. African indigenous knowledge and development policy. *INDILINGA- African Journal of Indigenous Knowledge Systems*, 1: 1-5.

Villani, S. 2006. *Mentoring and Induction Program that Support New Principals*. Thousand Oaks: California.

Wharton, L. 2000. *Moral leadership: A pipedream?* [Online]. Available: http//:www.leaders-values.com/content/detail.asp. [Accessed 22 March 2015].

Whitford, A.B., & Lee, S. 2014. Exit, Voice and Loyalty with multiple exit options: Evidence from the US Federal Workforce. *Journal of Public Administration Research and Theory*: pp.1-26.

Whitney, D., Trosten-Bloom, A., & Rader, K. 2010. Appreciative Leadership: Focus on what works to drive winning performance and build a thriving organisation. New York: McGraw Hill.

ENDNOTES

1. Peters T.J., & Waterman, R.H. 1982. *In search of excellence: Lessons from America's best-run companies*. Cambridge: Harper & Collins Publishers.

2. Bottery, M. 2004. *The challenges of educational leadership*. London: Paul Chapman.

3. Sergiovanni, T.J. 2000. *The life world of leadership: creating culture, community, and personal meaning in our schools*. San Francisco: Jossey-Bass.

4. Mthembu, D. 1996. African values: Discovering the indigenous roots of management. In R. Lessem., & B. Nassbaum (Eds.), *Sawubona Africa: Embracing Four Worlds in South African Management*. Sandton: Zebra, pp. 215-226

5. Mthembu, 1996. [See endnote 4]

6. Mbigi, L. 2005. *In search of the African business renaissance: an African cultural perspective*. Randburg: Knowledge Resources.

7. Mbigi, L. 1997. *Ubuntu: the African dream in management*. Randburg: Knowledge Resources.

8. Department of Education (DoE). 2001. *Manifesto on values, education and democracy*. Pretoria: Government Printer.

9. Ntuli, P. 1999. The missing link between culture and education: Are we still chasing Gods that are not our own? In M.W. Makgoba (Ed.), *African Renaissance*. Cape Town: Mafube, pp.184-199.

10. Ntuli, 1999. [See endnote 9.]

11. Dandala H.M. 1996. Cows never die: embracing African cosmology in the process of economic growth. . In: R Lessem, B Nassbaum (Eds.): *Sawubona Africa: Embracing Four Worlds in South African Management*. Sandton: Zebra, pp. 69-85.

12 Ntuli, 1999. [See endnote 9.]

13 Ntuli, 1999. [See endnote 9.]

14 Teffo, L. 1999. Moral Renewal and African Experience(s). In M.W. Makgoba (Ed.), *African Renaissance*. Mafube: Cape Town.

15 Teffo, 1999. [See endnote 14].

16 Maxwell, J.C. 1993. *Developing the leader within you*. New York: Thomas Nelson.

17 Maxwell, 1983. [See endnote 16].

18 Maxwell, 1983. [See endnote 16].

19 Maxwell, 1983. [See endnote 16].

20 Maxwell, 1983. [See endnote 16].

21 Maxwell, 1983. [See endnote 16].

22 Maxwell, 1983. [See endnote 16].

23 Mkandawire, T. 2005. Introduction. In T. Mkandawire, (Ed.), *African Intellectuals: Rethinking politics, Language, Gender and Development* (pp.1-9). London: Zed Books.

24 Teffo, 1999. [See endnote 14].

25 Teffo, 1999. [See endnote 14].

26 Ntuli, 1999. [See endnote 9.]

27 Teffo, 1999. [See endnote 14].

28 Msila, V. 2002. *Teachers as managers of Change*. Unpublished Doctoral Dissertation. Port Elizabeth: Vista University.

29 Maxwell, 1983. [See endnote 16].

30 Msila, 2002. [See endnote 28]

31 Makhanya, M.S. 2011. *Ethical servant leadership at UNISA*. Keynote address at the Principal's summit Royal Elephant Hotel, July 4, 2011.

32 Greenleaf, R.K. 2002. *Servant leadership: A journey into the nature of legitimate power and greatness*. New York: Paulist Press.

33 Masango, M. 2002. Leadership in African context. *Verbum et ecclesia*, 23 (3):707-718.

34 Masango, 2002. [See endnote 36]

35 Msila, 2002. [See endnote 28]

36 Hirschman, A.O. 1970. *Exit, Voice, and Loyalty: Responses to Decline in Firms, Organisations, and States*. Cambridge, MA: Harvard University Press.

37 Hirschman, 1970. [See endnote 42]

38 The Wallace Foundation 2007. *A Wallace Perspective: Getting Principal Mentoring Right: Lessons from the Field*. New York: The Author.

39 Villani, S. 2006. *Mentoring and Induction Program that Support New Principals*. Thousand Oaks: California.

40 Jazzar, M., & Algozzine, B. 2007. *Keys to Successful 21st Century Educational Leadership*. Boston: Pearson.

41 Scott, W.G. & T.R. Mitchell. 1976. *Organisation Theory: A Structural and Behaviour Analysis*. Homewood, IL: Richard D. Irwin.

42 Crafford, A. 2001. Communication. In S.P. Robbins., A. Odendaal., and G. Roodt (Eds.), *Organisational Behaviour: Global and Southern African Perspectives*. Cape Town: Pearson, pp. 223-240.

43 Crafford, 2001. [See endnote 48]

44 Crafford, 2001. [See endnote 48]

45 Hirschman 1970. [See endnote 42]

46 Hirschman 1970. [See endnote 42]

47 Hirschman 1970. [See endnote 42]

48 Miller, K. 2001. Values, Attitudes, and Job Satisfaction. In In S.P. Robbins., A. Odendaal., & G. Roodt (Eds.), *Organisational Behaviour: Global and Southern African Perspectives*. Cape Town: Pearson, pp. 65-84.

49 Dowding, K., Mergoupis, T., & Van Vugt, M. 2000. Exit, voice and loyalty: Analytic and Empirical developments. *European Journal of Political Research*, 37: 469-495.

50 Dowding, Mergoupis, & Van Vugt, 2000. [See endnote 55]

51 Whitford, A.B., & Lee, S. 2014. Exit, Voice and Loyalty with multiple exit options: Evidence from the US Federal Workforce. *Journal of Public Administration Research and Theory*: pp.1-26.

52 Dowding, K., Mergoupis, T., & Van Vugt, M. 2000. Exit, voice and loyalty: Analytic and Empirical developments. *European Journal of Political Research*, 37: 469-495.

53 Farrell, D & Rusbult, C.E. 1992. Exploring the Exit, Voice, Loyalty and Neglect Typology: The influence of job satisfaction, quality of alternatives and investment size. *Employee Responsibilities and Rights Journal*, 5(3): pp. 201-218.

54 Farrell & Rusbult, 1992. [See endnote 59]

55 Farrell & Rusbult, 1992. [See endnote 59]

56 Farrell & Rusbult, 1992. [See endnote 59]

57 Hirschman 1970. [See endnote 42]

58 Goman, C.K. 2004. "This isn't the company I joined": How to lead in a business turned upside down. National City, CA: KCS Publishers.

59 Goman, 2004. [See endnote 64]

60 Metz, T. 2011. *Ubuntu* as a moral theory and human rights in South Africa. *Africa Human rights law journal*, 11:532-559.

61 University of California San Francisco *Guide to managing human resources*. [Online]. Available:http:UCSfhn.UCSF.edu. [Accessed 2 May 2015].

62 Pio, E., Waddock, S., Mangaliso, M., McIntosh, M., Spiller, C., Takeda, H., Gladstone, J., Ho, M., & Syed, O. 2012. Pipeline to the future: Seeking wisdom in indigenous, Eastern and Western Traditions. In J. Neal (Ed.), *Handbook of faith and spirituality in the workplace: Emerging research and practice*. New York: Springer, pp. 195-222.

63 Martins, A.T. *12 simple ways to improve employees' productivity*. [Online]. Available:http://www.mytopbusinessideas.com. [Accessed 17 March 2015].

64 Bakke, D. *5 Effective time management tips. Techniques and skills you need to master*. [Online]. Available:http://www.moneycrashjers.com. [Accessed 13 March 2015].

65 Whitney, D., Trosten-Bloom, A., & Rader, K. 2010. Appreciative Leadership: Focus on what works to drive winning performance and build a thriving organisation. New York: McGraw Hill.

66 MindTools. *Successful delegation*. [Online]. Available: www.mindtools,com. [Accessed 28 March 2015].

67 Maxwell, 1983. [See endnote 16].

68 Mbigi, 2005. [See endnote 6]

69 Khoza, R. 1994. The need for an Afrocentric approach to management. In Christie, P., Lessem, R. and Mbigi, L. (Eds). *African management: philosophies, concepts and applications*. Randburg: Knowledge Resources: p.117–124.

70 Mbigi, L. & Maree, J. 2005. *Ubuntu: the spirit of African transformation management*. Randburg: Knowledge Resources.

71 Prinsloo, E.D. 1998. *Ubuntu* culture and participatory management. In Coetzee, P.H. and Roux, A.P.J. (Eds).*The African philosophy reader*. London: Routledge, pp.41–51.

72 Nel, C. 1994. Value-centred leadership – the journey to becoming a world-class. In P. Christie., R. Lessem., & L. Mbigi (Eds.), *African management: philosophies, concepts and applications.* Randburg: Knowledge Resources.

73 Maxwell, 1983. [See endnote 16].

74 Vilakazi, H. W. 2002. African indigenous knowledge and development policy. INDILINGA- African Journal of Indigenous Knowledge Systems, 1: 1-5.

75 Vilakazi, 2002. [See endnote 80].

76 Pityana, N.B. 2007. *Higher education, Transformation and Africanisation- A Paradigm Shift?* [Online]. Available: www.ieasa.studysa.org. [Accessed 10 August 2014].

77 Teffo, 1999. [See endnote 14].

78 Teffo, 1999. [See endnote 14].

INDEX

A

accountable employees work, 96
Africa, 3, 4, 38, 104–5
Africa leadership, 14
African communities, 52, 69
  humanism, 100
  languages, 4–5
  leadership, 104
  leadership modules, 104
  village, 4, 19, 64
agricultural science class, 3
application, 14, 50, 80, 81, 83
appreciative leadership, 88
aspirations, 45, 55, 87, 88, 103
attributes, 10–11, 32, 53

B

Barriers of communication, 43
behaviour, moral, 20, 21
belief, 4, 49, 56, 60, 94
brand, 23, 72, 73, 75, 76
breed unwilling workers, 74
business, core, 71–72

C

calabash, 52, 53
camaraderie, 52, 53
caring, 1, 3, 6, 56, 57, 105
challenges, 2, 29, 43, 50, 73, 76, 80, 81, 82, 104
change, 4, 6, 7–8, 10, 11, 18, 19, 20, 24, 42, 48, 56, 61, 104, 105
  agents, 8, 10, 31, 56
  cultures, 19
  face-to-face communication, 44

initiatives, 24, 103
  leading, 18, 104
  management, 18
  organisational culture, 18
  process, 24, 104
channels, strong communication, 75
civilization 105
climate, 6, 9, 17, 74, 94, 105
collaboration, 14, 45, 65, 82, 83, 96, 100
collegiality, 11, 39, 53, 57, 83
colonisation, 9
commitment, 4, 22, 30, 42, 54, 57, 67, 80, 84, 85, 94, 100–101, 104
collective, 72
  ploughing, 52, 54
communalism, 65, 102
communication, 9, 15, 37, 38, 39, 40, 41–45, 50, 65, 68, 82, 86, 90, 105
  characterises *ubuntu*, 39
  clear, 74
  effective, 38, 39, 40, 41, 42, 45, 68, 72, 82
  face-to-face, 44
  formal, 44
  good, 45, 82
  horizontal, 39
  internal, 39
  multi-directional, 39
  skills, 32, 43
  upward, 39
community, 1–4, 13, 14, 21–22, 38, 39, 40, 41, 42, 45, 52, 56, 57, 66, 100–103
conscientious, 3
culture, 99

117

ethic, 54
goals, 45
members, 6, 14, 21, 39, 40, 75
unified, 6
values, 4
working, 102
company, 6, 9, 39, 41, 44, 50, 51, 58, 62, 63, 71, 72, 94, 96, 99
company's management, 50
compassion, 21, 71, 73, 77, 100–101, 105
competition, 4, 6, 22, 73
  negative, 2
complimenting employees, 58
consensus, 6, 45, 62, 65–66, 68–69
corporate culture, 18
  changing, 19
  new, 18
criticise, 53, 54, 89
cultivator, 52
cultural
  backgrounds, 31, 38
  difference, 31
  values, 72, 73, 74
culture, 18, 19, 20, 24, 31, 32, 51, 74, 75, 78, 79, 82, 83, 92, 94
  changing, 18, 19
  conducive, 83
  manipulating, 18, 22
  organisation's, 83
  positive, 58, 81, 82
  right, 17, 80, 83
  ubuntu-inspired, 20
  upright, 21
culture and values, 51, 97
cultures and climate, 74, 94

D

decision-making, 9, 13, 62, 63, 65
decisions, 23, 57, 61–64, 66, 68, 72, 82, 92

collective, 33, 34, 61, 70, 80, 82
delegation, 90, 91, 92
developing change managers, 31
development, 6, 8, 11, 37, 79, 81
  collective, 102
  professional, 12, 75, 76
dignity, 42, 48, 75, 78, 79, 102
diligence, 25, 26, 78
direction, 32, 33, 39, 45, 66, 89
directors, 9, 40–41, 105
diversity, 21, 22, 31, 35, 70
duties, 2, 11, 84, 91
  delegated, 90, 92
dynamics
  cultural, 31
  understanding workplace, 28
dysfunctional workplaces, 6

E

education, 32, 104, 105
education system, 104, 105
effective cultures, 80
effective leaders, 2, 34, 35, 51, 52, 53, 56, 63, 67, 70, 76, 78, 103, 104
effective managers, 5, 14, 53, 54, 85–86, 92, 104
effective workplaces, 86
efficiency, 73, 74, 78
emotional intelligence, 92–93
empathy, 57, 58

employee, 10-11,19, 22, 25, 50, 54, 69, 80, 89,
  change, 10
  commitment, 54
  confidence, 89
  development, 22, 69
  expertise, 19
  isolation, 11, 50
  performance, 25, 80

employees, 9–10, 18, 24, 25, 30–34, 40–42, 48, 50–58, 67–70, 74–86, 89, 90, 91–93, 95, 102–5
  committed, 14, 17, 51
  compassionate, 26
  content, 23, 85
  diligent, 51, 85
  disgruntled, 76
  empowered, 22, 100
  equip, 27
  ethical, 96
  happy, 76, 95
  incentives, 90
  inspire, 50, 81
  loyal, 56
  new, 11, 86, 94–95
  nurture, 100
  producing, 14
  public sector, 49
  react, 23, 47
  reward, 83
  satisfied, 54, 89
  share management, 23
  spirit, 90
  strengths, 85
  strong, 57
  teaching, 50
  transcendental, 12
  treasure, 34
  turnover, 30
  unmotivated, 32, 74
ethical workers, 96
ethics, 21, 59, 69
eurocentric management styles, 10
EVLN model, 48, 49
excellence, 2, 4, 16, 73, 88, 101
excelling employees, 83
experience, 5, 12, 28, 29, 30, 50
  mentor-mentee, 30
exposing key leaders, 8
external communication, 39

F

facilitators of African leadership modules, 104
fellow employees, 12, 24, 51, 86, 93, 95, 103
fellow workers, 2, 6, 103
filtering, 43
Five Ps, 14, 15–17, 37, 47, 61, 71, 99
followers, 8, 12–13, 21, 25, 26, 48, 61

G

gifts, 14, 58
goals, 17, 94, 97
  set, 20, 97
group, 7, 14, 54, 62, 67, 82, 102
growth, 6, 7, 8, 12, 29, 31, 35, 78

H

helm, 16, 25, 56, 60
high performing teams, 95
hindrance, 31, 32
history, 32
honesty, 39, 40, 41, 42, 45, 78, 79, 86, 91, 96
humanness, 4, 5, 64, 69
human relations, 6

I

implications, 95, 96
improved organisational culture, 31
inability, 104
individualism, 2
information overload, 43
inspiring leaders, 26
institutions, 13, 83, 103, 104
intelligent leaders, 33
interconnectedness, 2, 3, 4, 5, 16, 99, 105

119

intercultural communication, 38
interdisciplinary project teams, 18

J

jobs, 21, 49, 74, 77, 90, 91, 99, 100

L

lazy employees, 85
leaders, 7, 12–16, 25–26, 33, 34–35, 45, 50, 52, 55, 56, 57, 58, 63, 77, 88
  affectionate, 57
  ambitious, 56
  bad, 41
  company, 79
  conscientious, 17
  creative, 53
  good, 34, 40, 48, 78
  inspirational, 33
  life-giving, 14
  strong, 74, 75
  transformational, 24, 25
  uncaring, 56
  unempowered, 25
  wise, 34, 53, 59
leadership, 6–7, 14, 21, 24, 34, 67, 70, 79, 86, 101, 104
  affectionate, 57
  appreciative, 88
  democratic, 24
  distributed, 23
  effective, 15
  ethical, 59
  good, 15
  models, 105
  organisational, 74, 90
  positions, 34
  qualities, 23, 55
  styles, 32
  transformational, 24, 35

leaders inspire, 25
leaders share, 14
level, 7–8, 10–11, 14
  five, 7, 10–11
life, 4, 5, 6, 14, 51, 99, 100
  way of, 1, 3, 4, 62, 100
listening, 18, 44, 55, 63, 69
love, 8, 9, 53, 79, 105
loyal, 8, 23, 25, 41, 47, 48, 50, 51, 52, 56, 57, 59, 62, 72, 78
  employees, 23, 52, 53, 54, 55, 57, 58, 60
  members, 54–57
  workforce, 56, 58
loyalty, 15, 21, 23, 47, 48, 49, 50, 51, 53, 54, 56–60, 62, 78, 99, 101

M

magnifying, 75, 76
management, 6, 9, 10, 11, 13, 14, 39, 56, 57, 82, 83, 85, 89–91, 100, 101
  collective, 78
  diversity, 31
  philosophy, 13
  practice, 5
  strategies, 5
  style, 9, 105
  team, 62, 65
  theory, 10
managers, 9, 18, 19, 23, 25, 44, 63, 65, 69, 79–86, 90, 91, 92, 97, 103
  best, 25
  circumstances, 50
  conscientious, 59
  good, 95
  matured, 104
  new, 18, 32
  visionary, 100
matured employees, 31, 93, 100, 103–4

Index

maturity, 6, 7, 10, 12, 22, 69, 93–95, 104
maximising productivity, 73
members, 15, 39, 41, 42, 43, 53, 56, 57, 59, 62, 68, 85, 87, 91, 100
mentees, 27, 28, 29, 30, 31, 32
mentor and mentees, 27, 29
mentoring, 26–27, 29, 30, 31, 32, 35, 86
  processes, 27, 29, 31, 32
  programmes, 30
  relationship, 27, 31
mentor-mentee relationships, 31
mentors, 9, 11, 27–32, 76, 105
  effective, 30, 31, 76
  good, 30, 31
models, 5, 7, 8, 10, 12, 25, 93, 100, 103
morals, 9, 21, 96
moral values, 21, 58–60
  shared, 59, 60
motivated employees, 26
motivation, 42, 74
  intrinsic, 79
moulding leaders, 8
multicultural societies, 5, 21, 31
mutual understanding, 64, 65

N

nation, 101, 102
nature, 27, 28, 41, 55, 66, 67
negative values, 57
neglect, 48, 49
  employees display, 23

O

old internalised cultures, 55
openness, 38, 39, 40, 45, 76, 79, 99, 101
organisational culture, improving, 80
organisational values, 51, 59, 60, 63
organisations
  communication, 39
  people-centred, 20, 23, 33
  productive, 101
  ubuntu-inspired, 33, 39
  working, 42, 83, 92, 100, 101

P

participation, 33, 37, 39
participatory leadership, 100
partisanship, 15, 17, 37, 47–49, 51, 53, 55, 57, 59, 61, 71, 72
passionate leaders, 24
paths, 13, 55, 87, 89
people-centred management, 22
People-centredness, 15, 17, 19, 20–21, 23, 24, 25, 26, 27, 29, 31, 33, 35, 71, 72
  model, 23
  workplace culture, 20
people-oriented leadership, 33
Permeable walls, 15, 17, 25, 37, 39, 40, 41, 42, 43, 45, 47, 61, 71, 72
philosophies, 3, 4, 9, 10, 28, 29, 31, 101, 105
pinnacle, 93–94
pivotal, 42, 99, 102
planning, 52, 84, 86
process, 6, 12, 16, 29, 30, 31, 79, 104, 105
production, 15, 17, 56, 58, 71, 72, 73, 74–81, 83, 84–87, 89, 91, 95, 96, 97
  delay, 76
  enhancing, 72, 79
  ensuring, 72
  low, 74
  people-centred, 80
  output, 73

productive employees, 75, 76
productive managers, 19
productivity, 50, 54, 62, 73, 74, 76, 77, 78, 79, 82, 93, 101
   bolster, 97
   drive, 75
productivity and efficiency, 73, 74
professional maturity and *ubuntu*, 103
Progeny, 15, 17, 37, 47, 61, 63, 65, 67, 69, 71, 72
programme, 77, 86, 89, 90
progressive workplaces, 3, 6
prosper, 2, 3, 33

Q

Quality, 94, 95

R

REAP values model, 96
relationships, 8, 40, 42
respected workers, 96
responsibilities, 8, 11, 20, 21, 23, 24, 91
revive workplaces, 16
rewarding employees, 58, 80, 83
rewards work, 79
roles, 10, 14, 15, 20, 57, 68, 71, 72, 79, 83, 100

S

season, 72, 100
selective perception, 43
selfishness, 6, 19, 20
servant leaders, 14
servant leadership, 13, 14, 16, 100
servant leadership defeats, 14
set, 20, 30, 63, 66, 76, 77, 97
   goals, 19, 30, 73, 81, 82, 92, 97

targets, 74, 75
vision, 100
shared leadership, 14, 83, 85, 86, 100, 102
shared moral values and loyalty, 58, 60
shared vision, 11, 17, 33, 54, 85, 86, 102
sharing challenges, 28–29
sharing *ubuntu* vision, 80
shift, paradigm, 6, 10, 105
skills, 24, 76, 77, 84, 89, 90, 92, 100, 102, 103, 104
   sharing, 86
SOAR analysis, 86–89
society, 5, 9, 13, 39, 40, 41, 66, 80
solidarity, 21, 22, 33, 34, 38, 39, 40, 42, 45, 47, 62, 64, 66, 67, 94–96
South Africa, 4, 5, 10, 13, 21, 22, 83
staff turnover, high, 56, 57
stakeholders, 38, 39
strengths, 18, 20, 22, 31, 73, 85, 87, 101
summit, 93, 95
survival, 3, 35, 54, 64
SWOT analysis, 86–88

T

teacher, 3, 10
team culture, 66, 82
team leadership, 24
team members, 20, 21, 38, 53, 66, 68
teams, 19, 20, 33, 34–35, 64, 66–69, 75, 76, 81, 82, 84, 91, 92, 95, 97
   building, 69
   diligent, 25, 90
   effective, 26, 67, 68, 69, 75, 76, 78
   employees, 77
   leading, 9

real, 66
strong, 66, 76, 85
winning, 83
working, 35, 67
theory, 3, 6, 9, 10, 14, 102
time, 52, 61, 75, 76, 78, 80, 83, 84, 85, 86, 89, 90, 91, 93, 95
effective, 78, 84
management, 83, 84, 85, 97
tools
right, 75, 76
working, 96
toxic workplaces, 3, 22
train, 70, 76, 86, 89
trainers, 86, 89
training, 30, 79, 82, 85, 86, 89, 91, 100
employees, 82, 90
transformational leadership, 24
leadership literature, 24
leadership style, 24
transparency, 39, 82, 86, 96, 99
trust, 24, 25, 33, 38, 53, 56, 59, 60, 68, 82, 86, 90, 91

U

ubuntu, 1–18, 20, 21–26, 32, 37–42, 45, 50, 51–52, 54, 57–58, 61–68, 71–76, 78, 79–82, 99–105
concepts, 102
driven organisation, 73
embracing, 101
inject, 5
live, 59
preach, 9, 105
support, 35
sustain, 3
time immemorial, 69
true, 73
leadership, 13–16, 23–24, 32, 34, 57, 70, 86, 88, 101
African values, 22
approaches, 101
vision guides, 81
characteristics, 70
context, 102
culture, 79–80
cycle, 13
demands, 105
factor, 5
ideals, 33
indigenous management, 73
inspired models trust, 25
leadership, 15, 88
management, 101
organisation, 82
paradigm, 99
practices, 6
communication, 41
creation, 6
spirit, 103
qualities, 2
styles, 70
support, 72
system, 41
workplace, 100, 101
workplace culture, 80
worldview, 39, 105
cycle, 4, 12, 13, 80
environment, 2, 43, 45, 72
philosophy, 6, 15, 25, 79
models, 9, 58, 80, 82, 85, 101, 105
values, 12, 25, 50, 59, 62, 63, 73, 74, 100, 101
principles, 12, 27, 34, 69, 80, 81
five Ps of, 3, 14, 15, 17, 37, 47, 61, 71, 101, 103, 104
values, 3, 4, 12, 16, 17, 20, 22, 42, 60, 62, 72, 73, 95–96, 100, 101
understanding, 9, 24, 28, 31, 32, 49, 63, 93, 95, 102
mutual, 64, 65–66, 95

V

village, 4, 14, 15, 19, 21, 23, 37, 38, 50, 62, 63, 72, 73, 75, 100
villagers, 14, 19, 21, 37, 38, 53, 63, 72, 100
vision, 21, 22, 33, 40, 41, 42, 59, 66, 67, 68, 69, 80–83, 86, 87, 103
  collective, 3
  common, 33, 102
  company's, 64
  organisational, 70
  organisation's, 72, 81, 83
  personal, 33
  sharing, 92
  ubuntu-inspired, 81
visionaries, 26, 59
voice and loyalty, 23, 47, 49

W

walls, 15, 39
weak employees, 57
western management and *ubuntu* indigenous management, 73
western management practice, 74
Western management tradition, 73
Western models, 9, 100, 103, 104

work, 17–18, 20–21, 25, 47, 48, 50, 55, 67, 73, 75, 76, 77, 81, 84, 91
  commitment, 54, 99
workers, 2, 3, 9, 10, 19, 20, 50, 51, 75, 77, 78, 85, 86, 89, 105
  gifted, 86
  motivated, 75
  ordinary, 63
  uncommitted, 79
work ethics, 6, 54, 83
working environment, 77
  best, 77

workplace culture, 79–80
workplace environment, 79
  good, 79
workplace experience, 78
workplace practice, 29
workplaces, 1–16, 18, 20, 21–22, 24, 28, 39, 50, 63–66, 71–74, 76, 78, 92, 94–96, 99–104
  affective, 57
  caring, 2
  excelling, 96
  good, 29
  managers, 9
  new, 19
  people-centred, 19, 22
  productive, 100
  supportive, 75
  tools, 76
  ubuntu-inspired, 3, 83, 102

www.ingramcontent.com/pod-product-compliance
Lightning Source LLC
Chambersburg PA
CBHW050830160426
43192CB00010B/1974